The Healers

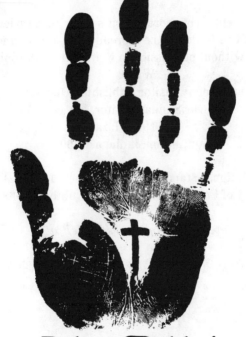

Robert Baldwin

Our Sunday Visitor Publishing Division
Our Sunday Visitor, Inc.
Huntington, Indiana 46750

International Standard Book Number: 0-87973-836-7
Library of Congress Catalog Card Number: 85-62815

Cover design by James E. McIlrath

PRINTED IN THE UNITED STATES OF AMERICA

836

To Annabelle,
Who Believed

Acknowledgments

I could not have written this book without the help of many persons. In particular, I am grateful to Mr. Robert Lockwood of Our Sunday Visitor, who first proposed the idea to me; to the Little Brothers of St. Francis in Boston; to the Father Solanus Guild in Detroit; to Catherine and William Odell of Mishawaka, Indiana — all of whom helped me locate needed reference material; and, above all, to my wife, Annabelle, whose patient and professional editing went into every chapter. Special thanks go to Mr. Daniel Naber of Providence for his encouragement, inspiration, and prayers. Finally, I am especially obliged to the Confraternity of Christian Doctrine for Scripture texts quoted verbatim or otherwise from the *New American Bible*, © 1970 by the Confraternity of Christian Doctrine, Washington, D.C., and to the Division of Christian Education of the National Council of the Churches of Christ for the use of Scripture quotations taken from the *Revised Standard Version Bible, Catholic Edition*, © 1965 and 1966 by the Division of Christian Education of the National Council of the Churches of Christ in the U.S.A., and used by permission of the copyright owners.

In addition, I am grateful to those publishers and others listed in the bibliography for the use of their materials. Among them are the Franciscan Herald Press, for excerpts from *Saint Francis of Assisi: Early Writings and Biographies*, by Marion A. Habig, © 1973; Doubleday Publishing Co., Image Books Div., for excerpts from *The Little Flowers of St. Francis*, by Raphael Brown, © 1958 by Beverly H. Brown; and The Catholic University of America, for excerpts from translations of the writings of St. Athanasius, St. Justin Martyr, Sulpicius Severus, and Tertullian, in *The Fathers of the Church*, © 1948—1954.

Contents

Preface

Throughout the history of the Catholic Church, certain persons have been credited with the ability to heal in extraordinary, if not miraculous, ways.

Our age, at least until recently, has not been friendly toward the miraculous. Most Catholics and, for that matter, members of mainline Protestant denominations have been distrustful of "faith healing."

In the twentieth century, however, attitudes have been changing. At this time in the Catholic Church there is a greater acceptance of the healing ministry than there has been for at least a thousand years. Catholics, as at no other time in recent history, are praying to God for healing and expecting that he will hear and answer their prayers.

God's willingness to answer prayers for healing is attested to in the Old Testament as well as in the Gospels, the Acts of the Apostles, and other books of the New Testament. Certain writings of the Fathers of the Church and the biographies of a number of saints also confirm what many believe to be instances of healing accomplished through prayer and faith.

There is nothing we could add to those writings

7

which would increase or decrease the credibility of those accounts. The purpose of this book is not to prove or disprove the authenticity of any of the thousands of healings attributed to Christian healers. There is nothing I could write that would persuade a confirmed skeptic to believe in miracles or a person of faith to abandon such belief. I would be happy if this book should convince a skeptic or two that God does answer prayers for healing, but that is not my aim.

My intent has been simply to show that the ministry of healing is an old and deeply rooted Catholic tradition, exercised both by ordinary Christians and by some of the greatest saints the Church has known.

To do this, I have assembled biographical sketches of Catholics who have exercised a ministry of healing at various times in the history of the Catholic Church. I have not included sketches of persons who are presently involved in the healing ministry but have concentrated instead on exploring how Catholics have healed in the past.

My purpose has been to show that the healing ministry, far from being a twentieth-century quirk of Pentecostals and charismatics, is actually a tradition founded by Christ and exercised by saintly Christians for nearly two thousand years.

— *R.F.B.*

Part One

The Roots of Christian Healing

1

The Healing Ministry of Jesus

"And Jesus went about all the cities and villages, teaching in their synagogues and preaching the gospel of the kingdom, and healing every disease and every infirmity" (Matthew 9:35).

It was Jesus himself who began the tradition of healing in the Church, and it was his own healing ministry that set the pattern for Christian healers who have been carrying on this ministry for nearly twenty centuries.

Healing, according to the gospel narratives of the New Testament, was a major part of Christ's ministry on earth. The four Gospels contain a total of 3,779 verses, and of these, 727 — nearly one fifth — deal either with the healing of physical or mental disorders or with the resurrection of the dead.

The fact that Jesus healed may even have been the biggest single reason that the multitudes were attracted to him. Everywhere he traveled, people came to hear him, to see him, to touch him. They pressed in on him until sometimes he found it necessary to slip away, alone, to pray. But even when he found the solitude he needed, the crowds were never far behind. In part, they were attracted by the way he taught, the excitement and hope of the good news he proclaimed: that the kingdom of God was at hand. Jesus was certainly a prophet and a teacher. But he was more. There were other men who prophesied and taught, but Jesus did things that no one else did — things that verified the good news that he spoke: he made people whole.

Sometimes he did it by touching them, sometimes by speaking to them. The eyes of the blind were opened, lepers were cleansed of their disease, and crippled people could walk again. At other times, the healing was spiritual: persons who had been "blind" were enabled by Jesus to see the reality of God's love and forgiveness. Sometimes Jesus encountered persons who were obsessed by fears and emotions that they could neither understand nor control — individuals who, today, would be called mentally or emotionally ill. In Christ's time, their obsessions and fears were seen as "unclean spirits." Jesus frequently freed such people from their fears and obsessions by commanding the spirits to depart.

The crowds marveled at his healing power, and eventually there were some who began to recognize it as a sign that Jesus was the long-awaited Messiah. Jesus himself cited his ability to heal as a sign of who he was. When John the Baptist (or Baptizer, as he is also called) — who had been preaching about the one who was to come — sent some messengers to Jesus to find out whether he was the Messiah, the messengers found Jesus curing the sick, casting out demons, and giving sight to the blind.

"Are you 'He who is to come,' or do we look for another?" they asked.

"Go back," Jesus said, "and report to John what you hear and see: the blind recover their sight, cripples walk, lepers are cured, the deaf hear, dead men are raised to life and the poor have the good news preached to them. Blest is the man who finds no stumbling block in me" (see Matthew 11:2-6).

But his purpose in healing wasn't to prove that he was God. In fact, he often warned those he healed not to tell anyone what had happened to them. Jesus healed for other reasons. He healed because he had compassion for those who suffered. He healed because he had his Father's love for humanity. In the fullness of his own humanity, he could feel and share the suffering of those who were sick. He healed because he wanted people to be well and he had the power to make them so.

In some ways, Christ's healing ministry reflected traditional Jewish attitudes about God, sickness, and health. But in other ways, it was radically different.

Judaism taught that God alone had the power to heal. The Jews saw health as a sign of God's blessing and sickness as a sign of God's displeasure. They believed that illness might result from transgressing moral laws or from violating one of the many Jewish dietary or purification rituals, that God punished people with curses and disease and rewarded them with blessings and good health.

The Jews recognized, however, that sickness sometimes afflicted even those whose obedience to God was unquestioned. The classic Jewish treatise on suffering, the Book of Job, explores the mystery of why a just and merciful God should allow innocent people to suffer. Its conclusion is that God's ways, even when they are incomprehensible to man, are right and just, simply because they are his.

That didn't mean that Old Testament Jews always accepted God's will without a struggle. If God chose to smite someone with illness, his motives weren't to be questioned; but a devout Jew could pray, repent, beg God for mercy, and even try to persuade God to soften his punishment.

One of the most endearing qualities of Judaism is the boldness and familiarity with which devout believers approach God. They don't question his power or wisdom, but they feel he is a God they can talk to, a God who entered into a covenant with his chosen people. He is approachable. It is possible to argue, even bargain, with him.

A good example of this occurs in the Book of Isaiah (38:1-5) when Hezekiah, king of Judah, pleads with God to spare his life. Hezekiah had been mortally ill when the prophet Isaiah came to him and declared, "Thus says the LORD: Put your house in order, for you are about to die; you shall not recover."

God had spoken. Hezekiah wasn't a man to question God's word, but he wasn't ready to die. He "turned his face to the wall and prayed to the LORD:

" 'O LORD, remember how faithfully and whole-

13

heartedly I conducted myself in your presence, doing what was pleasing to you!' And Hezekiah wept bitterly.

"Then the word of the LORD came to Isaiah: 'Go, tell Hezekiah: Thus says the LORD, the God of your father David: I have heard your prayer and seen your tears. I will heal you: in three days you shall go up to the LORD's temple: I will add fifteen years to your life.' " After that, Isaiah was able to heal Hezekiah with a poultice of figs.

The Jews not only believed that God healed in response to prayer but that he sometimes healed in inexplicable ways. In the fifth chapter of the Second Book of Kings, for example, when the army commander Naaman asks Elisha the prophet to cure his leprosy the prophet simply tells him to go wash seven times in the Jordan. Naaman, who had wanted something a bit more spectacular, becomes so angry and disappointed that he almost rejects Elisha's advice. Finally, he bathes in the Jordan and is cured. He returns to Elisha, humbled, and expresses his gratitude: "I will no longer offer holocaust or sacrifice to any other god except to the LORD," he said. The story of Naaman's cure, incidentally, doesn't end there. After Naaman is healed, his leprosy is transferred to one of Elisha's servants — as punishment for misconduct.

In our age, the healing of leprosy by bathing in a river would be considered so extraordinary that some people might call it miraculous. But to the Jews of the Old Testament, there wasn't a sharp distinction between "miraculous" and "natural" healing.

Their first response to illness wasn't to call a doctor, but to pray. Our age tends to look on the treatment of illness as strictly a "medical" problem. When we get sick, we visit a doctor. The ancient Jews prayed.

It is more than a coincidence that Old Testament healers like Isaiah and Elisha were prophets, not physicians. In other parts of the Middle East, the art of medicine was practiced; but it was too intertwined with magic, sorcery, and superstition to be readily accepted by the early Jews. In early Judaism, it was apparently considered a breach of faith to look only to physicians for healing. The Old Testament tells a story of how Asa, one of the kings of Judah, died because "even in his sickness he did not seek the LORD, but only the physicians" (2 Chronicles 16:12-13).

Some scholars say that the practice of medicine didn't even exist in early Judaism. At any rate, it wasn't as readily accepted among the Jews as it was in other parts of the ancient Middle East.

By the time Jesus began his public ministry, the Jewish people had become more tolerant of medical practice, probably through the influence of Greek culture. The Book of Sirach, written between 200 and 175 B.C. when Palestine was under Greek domination, clearly recognizes and proclaims that God uses physicians as instruments of healing. Its advice to the sick person is to pray, repent, make an offering to God, and, finally, to seek professional help:

> My son, when you are sick do not be negligent,
> but pray to the Lord, and he will heal you.
> Give up your faults and direct your hands aright,
> and cleanse your heart from all sin.

15

Offer a sweet-smelling sacrifice, and a memorial
portion of fine flour,
and pour oil on your offering, as much as you can
afford.
And give the physician his place, for the Lord created him;
let him not leave you, for there is need of him.
There is a time when success lies in the hands of
physicians,
for they too will pray to the Lord
that he should grant them success in diagnosis
and in healing, for the sake of preserving life.
He who sins before his Maker,
may he fall into the care of a physician.

— Sirach 38:9-15

But neither doctor nor prophet had ever healed the
way Jesus did. No one in the Old Testament had cured
so many people nor had any of the prophets healed with
so much authority. It wasn't necessary for Jesus to apply poultices or send lepers to bathe in the river. Often,
he simply told people they were well and it was so.

Like the Jews of the Old Testament, Jesus saw a
connection between sin and illness, but he was well
aware that sickness wasn't *always* the fruit of sin and
even when it was, he didn't insist that sinners reform
their lives before he would cure them. He hoped, but
never demanded, that those he made whole would re-
spond by reforming their lives and praising God with a
gratitude like Naaman's.

The four gospel narratives of the New Testament

16

record the separate and distinct healings of thirty-five individuals, not to mention ten instances in which "multitudes" and "great multitudes" are healed by Jesus. The only condition which he occasionally imposed was to ask those who wanted to be healed, "Are you confident I can do this?" His attitude wasn't that the sick should continue to suffer for their sins until they repented, but that they should know the love and power of God.

Yet on a number of occasions, he explicitly pointed out a connection between spiritual and physical health. "Remember, now, you have been healed," he once said to a cripple he had cured. "Give up your sins so that something worse may not overtake you" (see John 5:14).

To Jesus, sickness and sin went hand-in-hand; but so did healing and forgiveness. He forgave sins just as willingly as he healed, for he had the power and the desire to do both.

According to the Gospel of Matthew (9:1-8), on one occasion, in the Galilean town of Capernaum, some villagers brought a man to him who was paralyzed and lying on a mat. When Jesus saw their faith he said to the paralytic, "Have courage, son, your sins are forgiven." His exercise of such bold power was scandalous to certain scribes, authorities on Judaic law, who could not accept the idea of a man exercising authority that belonged to God alone.

"The man blasphemes," they said to themselves.

Jesus was aware of what they were thinking and said: "Why do you harbor evil thoughts? Which is less trouble to say, 'Your sins are forgiven' or 'Stand up and walk'? To help you realize that the Son of Man has authority on earth to forgive sins," he began, then turned away from them, faced the paralyzed man, and went on: "Stand up! Roll up your mat and go home."

The man did as he was told and and the crowd "praised God for giving such authority to men."

On that occasion and others, Jesus clearly revealed the connection between sin and sickness, but like the author of the Book of Job, he knew that sinners weren't the only people who got sick.

Once, on a Sabbath, Jesus encountered a man who had been blind from birth, and his disciples asked him, "Rabbi, was it his sin or that of his parents that caused him to be born blind?"

"Neither," said Jesus. "It was no sin either of this man or his parents. Rather it was to let God's works show forth in him."

Jesus then spat on the ground, mixed his saliva with the earth, and rubbed the mud on the man's eyes. At Jesus' command, the man departed to wash his eyes in the nearby pool of Siloam. Soon, he was back, able to see.

This particular healing, the subject of the entire ninth chapter of the Gospel of John, aroused the anger of some of the Pharisees, a group that placed supreme importance on observance of the Judaic law. They expelled the man from the temple, insisting that Jesus, who had the audacity to do such things on the Sabbath, was a sinner.

Unlike the Pharisees, the man who had been healed acknowledged Jesus as "the Son of Man" and bowed down to worship him. Jesus told him, "I came into this world to divide it, to make the sightless see and the seeing blind."

Some of the Pharisees overheard this and grew indignant. "You are not calling us blind, are you?" they asked.

Jesus told them, "If you were blind, there would be no sin in that. 'But we see,' you say, and your sin remains."

The Pharisees, like the scribes, were in a bind. On the one hand they correctly attributed all genuine healing to God. On the other hand, they were so committed to strict observance of the law that they could not accept Christ's healing as genuine.

They saw the same evidence of Christ's true identity that the messengers of John the Baptist had seen: the blind were recovering their sight, cripples were walking, lepers were being cured, and the deaf were hearing. Like John the Baptist, the Pharisees believed that God was the author of all healing, but unlike John they avoided the reality of who Jesus was. They saw Jesus as a sinner who was violating God's commandment to keep the Sabbath holy. Their problem was compounded by the fact that Jesus didn't merely heal as an intermediary between God and man — he himself exercised authority over illness, over sin, and over evil spirits.

When they were unable to disprove the authenticity of the healings, they sought to discredit the cures by depicting Jesus as someone who practiced sorcery — a serious charge to level against a fellow Jew.

"He is possessed by Beelzebul," some of the scribes asserted. "He expels demons with the help of the prince of demons." The name "Beelzebul" is commonly understood as a reference to Satan, but for the Jews it had additional connotations that were related to pagan idolatry, sickness, and healing. The name "Beelzebul" is a variation of "Baalzebub," the Old Testament name of a pagan god worshiped in the Philistine city of Ekron. The scribes were familiar with an Old Testament story (2 Kings 1) in which King Ahaziah, who briefly ruled Israel some eight hundred fifty years earlier, had been injured in a fall from a roof terrace. The king wanted to know whether he would be healed, but instead of trusting God, he sent messengers to seek an oracle from Baalzebub. His idolatry so angered God that he declared Ahaziah must die.

The scribes were therefore comparing Jesus with a former Jewish ruler who had sought favors from pagan gods. They may also have been trying to compare him with pagan medical practitioners who incorporated magic and sorcery. There is, in fact, a tradition in Talmudic literature that Jesus was put to death because he called on evil forces rather than God.

Not only was Jesus accused of using evil powers to heal but also of healing on the Sabbath. It seems likely that the two accusations were related. It is easy to imagine the scribes and Pharisees grumbling, "God wouldn't heal on the Sabbath — this must be from the devil!"

Jesus ridiculed the idea that his ministry was satanic. "If Satan is expelling Satan," he said, "he must be torn by dissension. How, then, can his dominion last? If I expel demons with Beelzebul's help, by whose help do your people expel them? Let them be the ones to judge you. But if it is by the Spirit of God that I expel demons, then the reign of God has overtaken you" (see Luke 11:18-20).

The expulsion of demons, like the curing of the sick, was an integral part of Jesus' ministry of making people whole. He regarded demons, or "unclean spirits," as evil, oppressive, and contrary to the wholeness that God desired for his people.

His attitude toward sickness appears to be much the same. The Church today recognizes that suffering can be a means to grace and teaches that some illness may even be given to us by God to help us grow. In the four Gospels, however, Jesus is no more tolerant of sickness than he is of unclean spirits.

It is, of course, possible to imagine Jesus telling a sick person, "Have courage, your Father is strengthening you and preparing you for a greater joy than you have ever known." Yet such statements are never attributed to him by the gospel writers. What they *did* write about, repeatedly, was his ability and desire to heal.

The idea that sickness might be the fruit of sin didn't deter him. He forgave the sin as easily as he healed the sickness. It is impossible to imagine Jesus telling a sick person, "You must continue to suffer because of your sins."

Because he was the incarnation of God, Jesus' healing ministry reveals God in a way that is sometimes hard to fully accept. He loves the sick and wants to relieve their misery.

Morton Kelsey, in his book *Healing and Christian-*

ity, goes so far as to declare, "The Christian who goes around saying that sickness is God's will has not fully understood the life and teaching of Christ."

To Jesus it was good to heal. During one of those controversial Sabbath healings he defended his actions on the basis of their goodness. In the synagogue, Jesus had encountered a man with a withered hand. Some Pharisees were keeping an eye on Jesus, ready to oppose him if he should be moved to heal the man. But Jesus disarmed them by addressing his critics before they had a chance to accuse him.

"Is it permitted to do a good deed on the Sabbath — or an evil one? To preserve life — or destroy it?" When no one spoke, he told the man to stretch out his hand. The man did, and his hand was perfectly restored (see Luke 6:6-10; Mark 3:1-5).

This particular healing was apparently a turning point for Jesus' enemies. When the Pharisees left the synagogue, they "immediately began to plot with the Herodians how they might destroy him" (Mark 3:6).

Within a short time, his enemies had him nailed to a cross, but that wasn't the end of Christ's ministry of healing. In fact, it was only the beginning.

2

The Healing Ministry
of the Apostles

One day in Jerusalem, about six or seven years after the death and resurrection of Jesus, an angry mob murdered a Jew "filled with grace and power, who worked great wonders and signs among the people."

The victim was a follower of Christ, fervently devoted to the new way of life proclaimed by Jesus. His eloquence in preaching the Gospel had stirred the anger of more traditional Jews.

His name was Stephen, and the story of his death is described in some detail in the seventh chapter of the Acts of the Apostles. It tells how his opponents, after accusing him of blasphemy, hauled him before the Sanhedrin, the Jewish council responsible for upholding Judaic law. As the council members glowered at him, "Stephen's face seemed like that of an angel." A more prudent person might have tried to talk his way out of such difficulties, but not Stephen.

Instead, he preached to them, accusing them of betraying and murdering Jesus in the same manner that their ancestors had persecuted the prophets. Those who were listening "ground their teeth in anger at him." Some of them undoubtedly wanted to kill him.

Legally, they couldn't. Jerusalem, at that time, was governed by Roman law. The Sanhedrin had the power to arrest and try Jews for alleged violations of Judaic law, but it did not have the authority to exercise capital punishment.

The onlookers, infuriated by Stephen's fervent devotion to the Gospel, suddenly rushed at him, dragged him out of the city and stoned him to death. Even as the stones battered him, he fell to his knees and prayed, "Lord, do not hold this sin against them."

At the edge of the crowd stood a young Pharisee named Saul. He was a zealous defender of the law and may have even been a member of the Sanhedrin. As a relentless enemy of the Church, he went along to see Stephen killed. He presided over Stephen's death in much the same way that a corrupt sheriff might preside at a lynching. No one who was there suspected that Saul was destined to become one of the best known healers of the early Church.

Later in his life, this zealous young persecutor of Christians would carry Christ's message of salvation throughout the Middle East and parts of Europe. He, more than anyone else, would define what it meant to be a Christian. He was to become not just an ordinary Christian, but an apostle — one of those chosen by Christ to teach the faith and preside over the new Church.

The apostles, among other things, were healers. Even before his death, Jesus summoned the twelve apostles he had chosen and "gave them authority to expel unclean spirits and to cure sickness and disease of every kind" (Matthew 10:1). Then he sent them out into the towns and villages to preach and to heal.

Yet the apostles weren't the only followers of Christ who healed. Similar powers were later bestowed by Christ on seventy other disciples and they too were sent out to preach and heal. But it didn't even stop there. On the eve of his crucifixion, Jesus indicated that, through the Holy Spirit, such extraordinary powers were to be exercised by all who believed in him.

"I solemnly assure you, the man who has faith in me will do the works I do, and greater far than these," he said. "Why? Because I go to the Father" (see John 14:12).

As the second chapter of Acts points out, that prophetic message probably wasn't understood very well by the apostles until the feast of Pentecost, some fifty days later. On that occasion, when all of them were gathered together, they were "filled with the Holy Spirit" and from that day forth began to proclaim the good news with renewed boldness and power. Jesus was no longer with them in the flesh but was with them through the power of the Spirit. And just as healing had been a characteristic of Christ's ministry on earth, it became, after Pentecost, one of the characteristics of the new Church.

Some modern Christians are uncomfortable with the healing ministry in the Church today, seeing it as irrelevant or of little importance to their faith. That was not the case among the members of the Church in the first century. They actively beseeched God to heal others through them: "Grant to your servants, even as they speak your words, complete assurance by stretching forth your hand in cures and signs and wonders to be worked in the name of Jesus, your holy Servant," they prayed (see Acts 4:29-30).

The Acts of the Apostles cites numerous miraculous healings as well as many "signs and wonders" worked by the apostles. There is strong evidence that the signs and wonders included additional healings.

Regularly, people brought sick persons to the apostles and, regularly, the apostles cured them. The Acts of the Apostles attributes some of the healings to Jesus' apostles in general and other cures to individual members of the Christian community. The apostle most frequently mentioned in connection with these miraculous healings is Peter.

Soon after Pentecost, as Peter and John were going up to the temple for the evening sacrifice they were confronted by a beggar who had been crippled from birth.

"I have neither silver nor gold," Peter told the man, "but what I have I give you! In the name of Jesus Christ the Nazorean, walk!" Then Peter took him by the right hand and pulled him to his feet. The man stood, then walked, then began leaping and praising God. Those who witnessed the healing were astonished (see Acts 3:1-10).

Another healing by Peter, according to Acts 9:32-35, resulted in many people being converted to the Lord. It occurred in a town called Lydda where the apostle healed a man named Aeneas who had been paralyzed and bedridden for eight years. All the inhabitants of Lydda and the neighboring town of Sharon were converted when they saw the man healed.

In another instance, Acts tells how people carried their sick into the streets on cots and mattresses, hoping that when Peter passed by, his shadow might fall on the sick and make them well.

But of all the healers of the early Church, the one of whom we know the most is the young Pharisee named Saul whom we met at the lynching of Stephen — the man whom Christians know as Saint Paul. He not only became a healer, but, as author of most of the New Testament, he wrote about the gift of healing and other gifts of the Holy Spirit.

What sort of man was Saint Paul? How was he transformed from a persecutor of Christians to perhaps the most influential Christian who ever lived? How did he manage to add his name to those of the original twelve apostles? How and why did he heal, and what do his writings reveal about the gift of healing?

There is a second-century description of Saint Paul as "a man of small stature, with his eyebrows meeting and a rather large nose, somewhat baldheaded, bandy-legged, strongly built, of gracious presence, for sometimes he looked like a man and sometimes he had the face of an angel." There is no way of knowing if the description is accurate, but its vivid details give it the ring of authenticity.

We do know that Saul — as we shall refer to Saint Paul for the moment — was born sometime at the beginning of the Christian era at Tarsus, an important city in what is now southern Turkey. It was a thriving port city with a university and was the home of many learned and wealthy families.

Saul and his family were members of the Diaspora, Jews scattered or dispersed from Israel. Such Jews continued to observe the Jewish law but also adopted, in varying degrees, some of the ways of the cultures in which they lived.

As citizens of Tarsus and Rome, Saul's family received certain legal privileges which the Jews of Israel lacked. They were proud of their Jewish traditions, and probably proud of their Roman citizenship too. Certainly they were more influenced by non-Jewish culture than the Jews of Jerusalem were. They shared the life and activities of their neighbors and fellow Roman citizens, but drew the line at things that involved idolatry, compromise with paganism, or moral laxity.

Because Saul was both a Jew and a citizen of Tarsus and Rome, he followed the common practice of having a Jewish name, Saul, as well as a Roman name, Paulus, or Paul. We know that as an adult, Saint Paul worked as a tentmaker (see Acts 18:3); but Scripture doesn't tell us whether this was a trade learned from his father.

His family was apparently well off, because when Saul was a young man he was sent to Jerusalem to complete his education as a student of Gamaliel, one of the greatest rabbis of that era. It appears from New Testament writings that he came to Jerusalem shortly after the death of Jesus.

He was a good student and impressed his elders

with his ability to expound the law. He learned the Old Testament by studying the Septuagint, the Greek translation of the Old Testament and other religious writings.

In Jerusalem, he became a Pharisee. The Pharisees were known by many Christians only as legalistic Jews who constantly sought to catch Jesus in violations of the Jewish law. But they were much more than that. They were more faithful than many other Jews in their religious devotions and they took worship seriously. They loved the Torah — the Law. It had been given to them by God through Moses, and they regarded it as a blessing. But some Pharisees were, indeed, legalistic and zealous, and Saul was one of them.

Zealous Christians like Stephen scandalized and enraged zealous Pharisees like Saul who regarded the Torah as the beginning and end of their faith. Saul believed that only through strict obedience to the law's many rules, regulations, and injunctions could God's people find salvation. Stephen and his fellow Christians taught that Jesus, not the law, was the source of salvation. To Saul, it seemed as if they were tearing apart all that was sacred.

As far as Saul was concerned, Stephen deserved to die. Saul didn't actually participate in the stoning: he guarded the coats of those who did the dirty work. Yet, as he watched the bloody event, Saul's own zealous nature must have been deeply stirred by the peaceful and faith-filled way in which Stephen accepted his death.

The controversy surrounding Stephen intensified the persecution that was directed against the Christian community in Jerusalem. The Christians scattered, many of them fleeing to the countryside. Saul, acting with authority given him by the Sanhedrin, harassed the Church — dragging men and women from their homes and throwing them into jail (see Acts 8:1-3).

It was while Saul was on his way to Damascus, to ferret out Christians who had fled there, that God intervened. This is how the ninth chapter of Acts describes the episode:

As Saul approached Damascus, a light from the sky suddenly flashed about him. He fell to the ground and at the same time heard a voice saying, "Saul, Saul, why do you persecute me?"

"Who are you, sir?" he asked.

The voice answered, "I am Jesus, the one you are persecuting. Get up and go into the city, where you will be told what to do."

The men who were traveling with Saul stood there speechless. They had heard the voice but could see no one. Saul got up from the ground unable to see, even though his eyes were open. They had to take him by the hand and lead him into Damascus.

Not yet baptized, Saul found shelter in Damascus at the home of a Christian named Judas. The New Testament tells us that Saul remained unable to see for three days. During those three days, the Lord appeared in a vision to a Christian named Ananias, telling him to go to the house of Judas where he would find Saul. Meanwhile, we are told, Saul had a vision too, in which Ananias imposed hands on him and cured him of his blindness.

Ananias, who knew the terrible reputation of Saul of Tarsus was, understandably, reluctant to follow the Lord's directive; but he did as he was instructed — not only healing Saul but baptizing him as well.

Saul's conversion is surely the most dramatic conversion in the history of Christendom, but it was only the beginning of his new life in Christ. Paul, the name by which he is best known to Christians, was convinced by his experience that he had seen the living Christ in the flesh. It was on the basis that Jesus had appeared to him and conversed with him that Paul claimed to be an apostle.

At first he visited synagogues, preaching to Jews who had not yet heard the Gospel of Jesus, as well as to existing communities of Jewish Christians. These communities were a minority group in the Jewish world; but Paul, as a Pharisee, was frequently welcomed as a speaker in the synagogues outside Jerusalem.

Then, some fourteen years after his first meeting with Peter, Paul says he returned to Jerusalem to meet not only with Peter but with the other leaders of the Church. His reason for going was to seek approval from the leaders of what Paul considered to be a mission revealed to him by God: the evangelization of persons who were not Jews.

In the end it was agreed that Paul and his companion Barnabas would serve as missionaries to the Gentiles, while Peter and the other apostles would continue to be missionaries to the Jews (see Galatians 2:1-10).

Once that role had been established for him, Paul threw himself fully into his role of spreading the Gospel throughout Asia Minor, Greece, and other Middle Eastern provinces of the Roman Empire.

Persecution of Christians by the Romans had not yet begun, and Paul, as a Roman citizen, was grateful to the Roman authorities for his ability to travel about in relative safety.

Yet Paul and Barnabas were frequently in trouble. Among the Jews, Paul's standing as a Pharisee would have added to his credibility, but his attitude toward the law was a threat to orthodox Judaism. The Jewish authorities in Jerusalem strongly objected to his insistence that salvation came through the risen Christ — that those who accepted Christ no longer had to depend on the law to be put right with God.

Paul also had opponents among some of his fellow Christians — Jews who saw Christianity as a new Jewish sect and who wanted to exclude the Gentiles, unless they were circumcised and lived according to the Mosaic law.

When he and Barnabas would arrive in a new town, they didn't know whether they would be welcomed, harassed, or simply ignored. Sometimes their opponents succeeded in barring the two preachers from the synagogues and sometimes they were able to get the Roman authorities to arrest the pair.

Paul and Barnabas preached to both Jews and Gentiles. Their preaching won new converts among some and stirred anger among others. In the Asia Minor town of Iconium, they spoke in the synagogue where they convinced "a good number of Jews and Greeks" (Acts 14:1). But a group of Jews who remained unconvinced opposed them and, with some of the town's Gentiles, planned to stone the two missionaries.

Paul and Barnabas fled to the nearby town of Lystra where they preached to the pagans. It was at Lystra that a remarkable public manifestation of Paul's gift of healing occurred.

One of the persons who heard Paul preach in Lystra was a crippled man who had been lame from birth. Acts 14:9-15 gives this account of how he was healed:

On one occasion he was listening to Paul preaching, and Paul looked directly at him and saw that he had the faith to be saved. He called out to him in a loud voice, "Stand up! On your feet!" The man jumped up and began to walk around.

The pagan crowds who witnessed this reacted very differently from the way a Jewish crowd would have.

"Gods have come to us in the form of men!" they cried. They began referring to the two missionaries as the pagan gods Hermes and Zeus, and the temple priest even brought oxen to sacrifice to them.

It was a sharply different reaction from the treatment they had received from their Jewish opponents and, in its own way, just as distressing. Paul and Barnabas tore their garments and shouted frantically, "Friends, why do you do this? We are only men, human like you. We are bringing you the good news that will convert you from just such follies as these to the living God, 'the one who made heaven and earth and the sea and all that is in them.' "

Paul isn't known primarily as a healer. He is, after Jesus, the most important teacher of Christianity, and it is for his teaching and his missionary activity that he is best known. His mission was to bring the good news to unbelievers and to encourage believers to persevere in authentic Christianity. But in the course of carrying out that mission, he was also a healer.

The Acts of the Apostles gives accounts of several other individual healings worked by Paul and at least one instance in which he is reported to have restored the life of a dead person.

At times, Paul's ability to heal was manifested in unusual ways. In Ephesus, when he ran into opposition in the synagogue, he simply departed with his disciples and continued his evangelization in a lecture hall where, we are told, "God worked extraordinary miracles at the hands of Paul. When handkerchiefs or cloths which had touched Paul's skin were applied to the sick, their diseases were cured and evil spirits departed from them" (see Acts 19:9-12).

That passage, incidentally, has served as a scriptural basis for the Catholic tradition of using the relics of saints in conjunction with prayers for healing; in addition, it is cited by some Pentecostals to explain the use of "prayer cloths" by certain persons who profess the ability to heal.

Although Paul is not known primarily for his own ability to heal and to cast out evil spirits, he apparently had a considerable reputation for this among his peers. So much so, in fact, that even some Jewish exorcists who had not accepted Christ tried to imitate Paul's methods.

These itinerant exorcists would command the spir-

34

its to depart by saying, "I adjure you by the name of Jesus whom Paul preaches." It didn't always work. On one occasion, the evil spirit is reported to have replied, "Jesus I recognize, Paul I know; but who are you?" (See Acts 19:13-15.)

Even when Paul was in captivity and being taken as a prisoner to Rome, he continued to heal. While he and his captors were shipwrecked on the island of Malta, they were guests of a man named Publius whose father was bedridden with chronic fever and dysentery.

Saint Luke, who apparently was present, describes what happened: "Paul went in to see the man and, praying, laid his hands on him and cured him. After this happened, the rest of the sick on the island began to come to Paul and they too were healed" (Acts 28:8-9).

Paul not only healed the sick but also wrote about the gift of healing in his letters to some of the Christian communities of his time. Those letters, which make up most of the New Testament, are the basis for our understanding of the healing ministry in the life of the Church.

To Paul, the gift of healing was one of the signs of an apostle. In fact, when some of the Christians at Corinth challenged his status he reminded them of the "signs and wonders and deeds of power" he had worked in their midst. These, he said, were among the signs of an apostle (see 2 Corinthians 12:12).

It is interesting to note that Paul wasn't merely *claiming* to have done these things, but *reminding* the Corinthians of things he had done when he was among them. Had his claims been false, he would have utterly destroyed his credibility in that community.

Although he doesn't specifically say which signs he is referring to, it can be inferred that they included healing. (The Greek words which Paul used for signs, wonders, and deeds of power are frequently used in the New Testament in connection with miraculous healings. Readers who wish a detailed examination of this point can find it in Chapter Six of *Healing and Christianity*, by Morton T. Kelsey.)

Even though Paul considered such deeds of power to be among the signs of an apostle, he did not consider the gift of healing something that Christians could be proud to possess. It was not an ability that believers earned or mastered by their own efforts, but one of a variety of gifts freely given to believers by God through the Holy Spirit.

"Now there are varieties of gifts, but the same Spirit [Paul explains in his First Letter to the Corinthians]; and there are varieties of service, but the same Lord; and there are varieties of working, but it is the same God who inspires them all in every one. To each is given the manifestation of the Spirit for the common good. To one is given through the Spirit the utterance of wisdom, and to another the utterance of knowledge according to the same Spirit, to another faith by the same Spirit, to another gifts of healing by the one Spirit, to another the working of miracles, to another prophecy, to another the ability to distinguish between spirits, to another various kinds of tongues, to another the interpretation of tongues. All these are inspired by one and the same Spirit, who apportions to each one individually as he wills" (12:4-11).

3

Early Christian Healers — From Egypt to Gaul

During the Church's first three hundred years it was dangerous to be a Christian. The first generation of believers, as we have seen, faced active and sometimes violent opposition from within the Jewish community. Later generations faced even more intense persecution from Roman emperors, who punished Christians with imprisonment, torture, death, or exile.

The Roman persecutions began about the middle of the first century, probably during the reign of Nero Claudius Caesar. After fire destroyed much of Rome in the year 64, Nero made a scapegoat of the Christian community. According to the Roman historian Tacitus, "Nero fastened the guilt and inflicted the most exquisite tortures on a class hated for their abominations, called Christians by the populace. . . ."

As time passed, the hatred of Christians spread.

Nero's persecution had been directed primarily against the Christians in Rome, but the emperor Domitian extended it throughout the empire. Furthermore, he demanded that his subjects treat him as a god — an impossible demand for the followers of Jesus.

Following Domitian's reign, persecution came in waves. Under certain emperors, Christians might be tolerated for a time; but, as members of a forbidden sect, they knew that sooner or later another emperor would arise to make them, once again, a political scapegoat.

Jesus himself had foretold such persecution but had assured his followers that those who endured it in faith would inherit eternal life. The cruelty of the Roman emperors challenged that faith; but, in those times, Christianity didn't attract halfhearted believers. Their belief in the resurrection was stronger than their fear of death.

And so, in the midst of persecution, the underground Church thrived and grew. It was a Church rich in the gifts of the Holy Spirit, and its members were confident that with faith in Jesus they could move mountains. They traveled to the ends of the empire, spreading their forbidden faith and bringing new hope and light to parts of Europe, the Middle East, North Africa, and Asia. Moreover, according to ancient Church writings, these early Christians carried the gift of healing with them.

Our knowledge of how they exercised their healing ministry is limited. Most of what we know of the Church in this period comes from the writings of the Fathers of the Church. These were theologians who sought to continue the teaching of the apostles and to resolve theological problems that arose as the Church expanded. But they were not historians. They wrote for the Christians of their time, not ours. It was their expectation that Jesus would return soon, so they were not concerned about preserving records for the benefit of future generations. As a result, they left no detailed descriptions of the healing ministry as it existed in the early Church. When they wrote about healing, it was in an almost casual way, as if it were simply an accepted part of ordinary Christian experience.

Justin Martyr, Origen, Cyprian, and Tertullian are among the Fathers of the Church whose writings mention healing and the related ministry of exorcism — the expulsion of demons who were believed to cause mental and physical disorders.

Justin Martyr, a convert who taught philosophy in Rome until he was killed by the Romans around 165, was a well-educated man from a pagan and Greco-Roman background whose interest in philosophy eventually led him to study the teachings of the Jewish prophets and of Jesus. He became a Christian about thirty-five years before his martyrdom.

One of his writings, known as the *Second Apology*, was addressed to the Roman Senate in the middle of the second century as a defense of the Christian faith. In the sixth chapter, he explains how Jesus "was born in accordance with the will of God the Father and for the benefit of believers, and for the defeat of the demons."

He goes on: "Even now, your own eyes will teach you the truth of this last statement. For many demoniacs throughout the entire world, and even in your own city, were exorcised by many of our Christians in the name of Jesus Christ, who was crucified under Pontius Pilate; and our men cured them, and they still cure others by rendering helpless and dispelling the demons who had taken possession of these men, even when they could not be cured by all the other exorcists, and exploiters of incantations and drugs."

Tertullian, converted at Carthage in North Africa, was another of the Church Fathers whose writings reveal something about the healing ministry in the early Church. Near the beginning of the third century, he wrote a letter to Scapula, a local Roman official who had launched a bitter persecution of Christians.

In the letter, Tertullian tried to persuade Scapula to stop the persecution. He asserts in the letter that some Roman officials, while publicly opposing Christians, were privately going to them to seek prayers for healing. He writes:

> All these things you may learn from the officials on your staff, from the same advocates who themselves have benefited from the Christians, although in court they vote as they like.
>
> For the secretary of a certain gentleman, when he was suffering from falling sickness caused by a demon, was freed from it; so also were a relative of some of the others and a certain little boy. And heaven knows how many distinguished men, to say nothing of common people, have been cured either of devils or of their sicknesses.

40

Even Severus himself [the emperor Septimus Severus], the father of Antonius, graciously remembered the Christians. He searched for Proculus — a Christian whose surname was Torpacion, a manager in the employ of Euhodia — who had cured him once by means of oil, and kept him in his palace until his death.

The practice of anointing with oil, combined with prayers for healing, was apparently common in the early Church. It has its scriptural basis in the New Testament: "Is any one among you suffering? Let him pray. Is any cheerful? Let him sing praise. Is any among you sick? Let him call for the elders of the church, and let them pray over him, anointing him with oil in the name of the Lord; and the prayer of faith will save the sick man, and the Lord will raise him up; and if he has committed sins, he will be forgiven. Therefore confess your sins to one another, and pray for one another, that you may be healed. The prayer of a righteous man has great power in its effects" (James 5:14-16).

The practice of anointing in the modern Church is known as the *Rite of Anointing and Pastoral Care of the Sick*. Although that sacrament is exercised today only by the clergy, it is interesting to note that in Tertullian's time lay Christians were apparently using this rite to heal one another — and pagans as well.

It was as natural for early Christians to heal as it was for them to preach the good news, suggests Kelsey, who notes that the early Christians saw illness as the work of Satan. He concludes, in *Healing and Christian-*

ity, that "healing was rescuing men from the domination of the enemy. This was the natural function of Christians as members of the body of Christ."

Toward the end of the period of Roman persecution, a new phenomenon arose in the Church, the first stirrings of a movement that was to produce many Christian healers in the centuries to come. The movement was monasticism, and its early Christian roots were planted in the sandy soil of the northern Egyptian desert. It was here that certain Christians began to seek a deeper experience of God through solitary prayer and fasting. Emulating Christ's own period of fasting in the wilderness, they sought the stillness of the desert. For these prayerful hermits, God was the only reality that mattered. And among them the gift of healing was very much alive.

These early Christian monks — known as the desert Fathers — spent their lives praying and fasting but didn't write about it. They taught their disciples directly, without books. What we know about them comes from the reports of others — writers who visited their communities and wrote about what they saw there. Many marvelous signs and wonders, including miraculous healings, are attributed to these desert contemplatives. It is difficult to separate fact from fiction in some of these accounts which may have been retold many times before they were written down. Some modern scholars, reluctant to accept the reported miracles as fact, have simply dismissed them as pious legends.

But the best-known written record of monastic life

in the Egyptian desert comes to us from a sober, well-educated Christian leader who wrote a biography of the most influential of all of the desert Fathers. The writer was Saint Athanasius the Great (c. 297-373), bishop of Alexandria, and the man he wrote about was Saint Anthony, Abbot (also called Saint Anthony of the Desert).

Anthony was born in northern Egypt in about 251, a son of fairly wealthy Christian parents. The family belonged to the Coptic church, a Christian sect which retained elements of an older Egyptian faith. Christianity had come to northern Egypt with little conflict, and pious Copts like Anthony's father had thus far escaped the persecutions suffered by Christians in other parts of the empire.

Yet even in Egypt, Christians were a minority and wary of the pagan customs that surrounded them. Anthony's father didn't send his son to school but encouraged him in a life of prayer and protected him from Greek influences. According to Athanasius, Anthony's only human contacts as a child were with members of his family. He was utterly unprepared for any kind of worldly life when, at about the age of twenty, his parents died, leaving him responsible for the family's lands and the care of his younger sister.

He remembered the gospel story of the rich young man whose attachment to possessions had prevented him from following Christ. So Anthony, being a pious youth, did what Jesus had urged the rich young man to do. He sold all the property he had inherited and gave it to the poor. He entrusted the care of his sister to a community of "virgins who were well known and faithful"

43

and who lived in what was apparently a convent of some kind.

Anthony chose to live in solitude, camping near his own village. He sought out other devout hermits for their advice and example in living a virtuous life and "directed his whole desire and all his energies to strengthening his spiritual practices." The villagers liked him and treated him affectionately.

As Anthony grew spiritually, he was drawn into battle with the forces of darkness. Many Christians today give little thought to the reality of the devil as a person, but he was real enough to Anthony. Jealous of Anthony's virtue, the devil began to distract him with worries about his sister and to tempt him with visions of money, food, and sexual pleasures. But by praying, fasting, and meditating on Christ's saving love, Anthony defeated the devil in all these battles.

To prepare himself against further diabolic attacks, he undertook severe fasts and rigorous physical disciplines. In denying his body comfort, he declared that "the state of the soul is vigorous when the pleasures of the body are weakened."

For nearly twenty years, Anthony and the devil fought each other. During that time, Anthony remained in seclusion at an abandoned fort in the desert. Frequently, friends would come to visit him, but he would make them remain outside where they were horrified by the shrieks and screams coming from within. On one occasion, some visiting friends became so alarmed by the noises that they looked inside. There they could see no one but Anthony, who calmly sent them away, telling them to make the sign of the cross and to have no fear.

When these years of spiritual warfare ended, Anthony emerged from his fort and was at peace. Many people, drawn by the stories they had heard of him, went into the desert to see this extraordinary hermit. They were impressed by his calm nature. It seemed to them that he had the placid assurance of a person filled with the spirit of God.

It is at that point in Anthony's life that Athanasius begins to relate some of the miraculous healings attributed to the saint. The major part of the biography is devoted to Anthony's teachings, admonitions, and exhortations to holiness; but his healings and exorcisms are recorded too.

Among those who came to see Anthony were people who were sick or troubled. "Through him," Athanasius writes, "the Lord healed many of those present who were suffering in body and freed others from evil spirits."

In one episode he tells how Anthony was visited in his cell by a man named Martinianus, a military officer whose daughter was troubled by an evil spirit. Martinianus knocked repeatedly, but Anthony, who valued his solitude, refused to open the door.

"Man, why do you keep crying out to me?" Anthony shouted. "I am only a man like yourself. If you believe in Christ, whom I serve, go, and according as you believe, pray to God and it will be done." So Martinianus prayed, and his daughter was made clean.

In another story Athanasius tells of a man named Fronto, afflicted with a disease which caused him to bite his tongue and in some manner endangered his eyesight.

"He came to the mountain and asked Anthony to pray for him," Athanasius writes. "After he had prayed, Anthony said to Fronto: 'Go, now, and you shall be healed.' "

But when Fronto, not yet cured, insisted that Anthony continue to pray, Anthony told him, "You cannot be healed while you remain here. Go away, and when you reach Egypt you will see the sign which is being done in you."

Fronto left, and when he came within sight of Egypt "he was cured of his disease and made well, according to the work of Anthony which he had learned from the Saviour in prayer."

Anthony's attitude toward healing is summed up by Athanasius in this manner:

> He sympathized and prayed with those who were suffering, and the Lord often heard him, as he showed in many ways. When he was heard, he did not boast, nor did he murmur when not heard, but he always gave thanks to the Lord and encouraged the sufferers to be patient and to know that healing belonged neither to him or any man, but to God alone who works when he wills and toward whom he wills.

> The sufferers therefore received even the words of the old man as healing, having learned not to be downcast but rather to suffer in patience, and those who were cured learned not to thank Anthony but God alone.

And yet it was through the man Anthony that God worked. As Athanasius goes on to say:

> We must not doubt that these many wonders were performed by a man, for it is the promise of the Saviour who said: "If you have faith, like a mustard seed, you will say to this mountain, 'Remove from here,' and it will remove. And nothing will be impossible to you." And again, "Amen, amen, I say to you: if you ask the Father anything in my name, he will give it to you. Hitherto you have not asked anything in my name. Ask and you shall receive." And it is he who said to his disciples and to all who believe in him: "Cure the sick, cast out devils, freely you have received, freely give."
>
> Accordingly, Anthony healed, not as one commanding but by praying and by calling on the name of Christ, so that it was evident to all that he was not the doer, but the Lord, who through Anthony, showed his love for mankind and healed the suffering. Only the prayer was Anthony's and the self-denial for the sake of which he had settled on the mountain, where he rejoiced in divine things.

Not everyone who came out to Anthony's desert fort was seeking healing. Some came looking for his guidance so that they too might overcome the power of the devil and devote their lives to praying, fasting, singing psalms, and praising the Lord. A community of disciples grew up around Anthony. He taught them to love solitude and to find God in the stillness of their hearts and, when he thought they were ready, he departed from them, moving deeper into the desert.

Even there, people continued to seek him out. Eventually, his disciples numbered in the thousands. In his remote cave Anthony was once again surrounded by people clamoring for his instruction. Once again he put aside his yearning for solitude and taught a new wave of disciples. Then he moved to a cave still deeper in the desert.

This time his quest for solitude was interrupted by the Roman Empire's last great persecution of the Church. News reached Anthony that Christians by the hundreds, in Alexandria, were being tortured and burned for their faith or fed to wild beasts to amuse the crowds in the arena. Anthony, who for decades had fought Satan in solitary spiritual combat, realized that the time had come when he was to face his old enemy again — this time in the world of men. Anthony, then about sixty years old but tough in body and strong in spirit, left his desert hermitage and traveled to Alexandria, ready for battle.

He went among the faithful — in prison and in the courts of law — encouraging them in their faith and willingness to die for Christ. The authorities, determined to put an end to this, gave orders that no monk was to appear in the court or even to remain in the city. Anthony didn't mind that his life was in danger. In fact, he prayed that he too might become a martyr. Fearlessly he walked where he pleased and continued to go among the Christian prisoners, in plain view of the prefect. The authorities, dumbfounded by Anthony's calm fearlessness, did not harm him. The desert hermit remained in Alexandria until the persecution came to an end in 312. We don't have many details on how this was accomplished, but Anthony's nonviolent resistance was surely a factor.

Probably by this time, the Roman authorities were beginning to realize that the Church was too well established to be destroyed. The end of the persecution in Alexandria marked the end of an era. Never again would the empire seek to destroy Christianity through genocide.

The following year, a new emperor, Constantine, had an experience which led directly to official tolerance of Christianity throughout the Roman Empire. Constantine, who was preparing for a battle against a rival, had been unsuccessfully asking his god Apollo to give him a sign of victory in the fight. Instead of a sign from Apollo, Constantine had a vision of a flaming cross, beneath which were inscribed the words, "By this sign you will conquer." Constantine, in defeating his enemy, was convinced that the God of the Christians had given him the victory.

In 313, Constantine issued the Edict of Milan declaring that the adherents of the various religions of the empire, including Christianity, were henceforth free to worship as they pleased.

Although Constantine had been impressed with the God of the Christians, he was not yet a Christian himself. It wasn't until some twenty-five years later — on his deathbed — that he was baptized. But his edict changed the course of history. What had been a forbidden sect went on to become, in a relatively short time, the official religion of the Roman Empire.

Soon the Church was winning thousands of new converts, but in doing so, the Church changed. Its new members were people whose faith had never been tested by the threat of torture and martyrdom. Ordinary Christian life became not only less dangerous but less zealous. The average Christian didn't strive, as the apostles and martyrs had, to live holy lives in total obedience to God.

Not surprisingly, as apostolic zeal diminished, the gift of healing and other charismatic gifts diminished too. But they didn't disappear altogether. God continued to heal through the sacraments of the Church and through the ministry of particular Christians whose zeal was undiminished. Such a Christian was Saint Martin (316-397), bishop of Tours.

He was born soon after the Edict of Milan in what is now a part of western Hungary, but he was raised in northern Italy. Most of what we know of him comes from a biography written by Sulpicius Severus, a Christian writer who became a friend of the saint toward the end of Martin's life.

The healings and miracles attributed to Martin by Sulpicius were a subject of controversy among the churchmen of his time, and they continue to be questioned by some scholars today. Whether or not they are true, they were widely enough accepted at the time they were written to help us understand Church attitudes toward healing in the fourth century.

Like Anthony, Martin was an ascetic who devoted

himself to rigorous spiritual exercises. But many of the bishops of his time advocated a less intense spirituality and apparently were suspicious of Martin and his miracles.

Sulpicius, in the first chapter of his *Life of St. Martin*, seems aware that the biography would be challenged. He declares that Martin, "looking for no praise from men," would have "wished to conceal all his miracles, insofar as he could."

He continues, "Even so, among those acts of which I have learned, I have omitted many, thinking it sufficient if only the outstanding ones should be noted. Consideration for my readers required me at the same time to see to it that an excessive mass of material should not weary them. I beg those who will read this to give their trust to what has been written, and to believe that I have set down nothing without full knowledge and proof. Rather than tell falsehoods, I should have preferred to be silent."

Martin was the son of pagans but was attracted to the Christian faith. When he was fifteen he was still unbaptized but had decided he wanted to become a monk. His father opposed him in this and turned him over instead to be trained as a soldier in the service of Emperor Constantius II.

He became not only a soldier but also a catechumen preparing for baptism. He was well liked by his comrades, who observed and respected his moral and conscientious manners.

The most famous story about Martin comes from his army days. During a particularly cold winter while

Martin was walking through a village, he encountered many people so poor that they didn't have enough clothes to keep them warm. Bit by bit, Martin began giving away the clothes he was wearing. When he had nothing left but his armor and a simple military cloak, Martin encountered a naked pauper. Many people had passed by the poor man, ignoring his condition, but Martin took off his cloak and with his sword cut it in half, giving half to the pauper and keeping the other half for himself. Some bystanders laughed at Martin and the pauper — each trying to cover himself in half a cloak. Others among them felt a pang of remorse, realizing that they too could have helped the pauper but had done nothing.

That night, Jesus appeared to Martin in a dream — wearing half a cloak. Martin was deeply moved by this experience which underscored for him the meaning of Christ's words: "Whatsoever you do to the least of my brothers, you do to me." He was baptized without further delay.

After his baptism, Martin felt that armed combat was not permissible to him as a Christian — and he won his release from the military.

Soon after, he sought out Hilary (c. 315-368), bishop of Poitiers, known to Martin for his steadfast faith. Hilary wanted to make him a deacon, but Martin resisted, insisting he was not worthy. Hilary asked him to become an exorcist, a lower order of clergy. For some years, Martin served the Church in this role. Eventually, he established a monastery at Milan but was driven out of the city by the local bishop, who had embraced the Arian heresy — a doctrine that recognized Christ as the head of the Church but denied that he was coequal with God the Father. Later, near Rome, Martin set up another monastery and it was here that his first healing miracle is recorded by Sulpicius.

Returning from a journey, Martin learned that during his absence, one of the members of the community — a man preparing for baptism — had died. Sulpicius writes that Martin sent the other brothers away, barred the door, "stretched himself upon the lifeless body of the dead brother," and prayed.

"Hardly two hours had elapsed before he saw all the limbs of the dead man move little by little and his eyes quiver as they opened, once more to see," Sulpicius continues. "Then, turning to the Lord with a loud voice and giving thanks, Martin filled the whole cell with his cry of joy. On hearing this, those who had been standing outside the door at once rushed in. Wonderful spectacle: They saw alive one whom they had abandoned as dead."

By the time of that incident, Martin was already regarded as a saint, but "he was now regarded as powerful in wonders and truly apostolic." His popularity grew and led to his election as bishop of Tours in Gaul in about 370, despite the active opposition of some powerful Church leaders.

He continued to devote his life to prayer and fasting, and stories began to circulate about his ability to heal the sick and to perform other miracles. "In the matter of healing," Sulpicius writes, "Martin had such a power of grace within him that hardly anyone who was

sick approached him without at once recovering health."
A typical healing story told by Severus is this:

> At Treves [Trier], a girl lay ill in the grip of a
> fearful paralysis. For a long time, she could make
> no use of her body for the needs of human life.
>
> Already dead in all her members, her body
> breathed feebly and barely pulsed with life. Her
> kin were standing by, awaiting only her funeral,
> when suddenly the news was brought that Martin
> had come to that city. When the girl's father
> learned this, he ran breathlessly to beseech him on
> behalf of his daughter. As it happened, Martin had
> already entered the church. There, under the eyes
> of the people and many other bishops, the old man,
> waiting, embraced [Martin's] knees and said, "My
> daughter is dying from a terrible kind of sickness.
> Her condition is more cruel than death itself: it is
> only through breathing that she lives; in her flesh
> she is already dead. I beg you to come to her and
> bless her, for I have faith that she can be restored
> to health through you."
>
> These words confused and astonished Martin
> and he drew back, saying that the grace required
> for such an act was not his. The old man's judg-
> ment had misled him, he said; he was unworthy to
> be a manifestation of the Lord's power. The father
> persisted, weeping more bitterly and praying him
> to visit the lifeless girl. Finally, the bishops who
> stood about compelled him to go and he went down
> to the girl's house. A great crowd was waiting

before the door to see what the servant of God would do. Using means which were familiar to him in situations of this kind, he first prostrated himself upon the floor and prayed. Then he looked at the sick girl and asked that some oil be given him. He blessed the potent and sanctified fluid and poured it into the girl's mouth. At once, her voice was restored to her. Then, at his touch, her members one by one began gradually to regain life until, with the people there to witness it, strength returned to her limbs and she arose.

There is no way of proving or disproving the miracles attributed to men like Anthony and Martin. We cannot go back in time to interview the people they are reported to have cured. Nor can we say for certain whether these stories are factual history or pious legend. But we do know that among some of the best-known churchmen of their day, these stories were considered worthy of belief. And we know this: that Jesus had told us to expect such things among those who came after him.

Part
Two

An Enduring Tradition

4

Sacraments, Relics, and Shrines

There is much evidence of a flourishing healing ministry among the Christians of the first three centuries, but after that the record is not so clear.

As we have seen, the healing miracles of Saint Anthony and Saint Martin were attributed to them by authors who were respected churchmen with personal knowledge of the men about whom they wrote. The healings attributed to the saints of the next several centuries were from more obscure sources.

Many legends and stories tell of miracles worked through the great missionary saints who spread Christianity throughout Europe, but it is impossible to know how much of this information is reliable. Reports of marvelous healings exist side by side with tales of Saint Patrick banishing snakes from Ireland or Saint George slaying the dragon. The stories have their own charm but are simply not reliable as historical information.

Some interpreters of Church history believe that

the gift of healing and other charisms were given by God to the apostles to help the Church become established. According to that view, the gifts disappeared in later centuries because they were no longer needed.

Catholic writings indicate that healing continued to occur in the Church — sometimes through the ministry of individual Christians but more often in other ways. From the fourth century through the Middle Ages, it appears that Catholics sought healing primarily through sacramental anointing or through visits to shrines where the bones or other relics of the saints and martyrs were kept.

The veneration of the remains of departed Christian heroes began at least as early as perhaps 156, believed to be the year when Saint Polycarp was burned at the stake in Smyrna (present-day Izmir). The Christians of Smyrna gathered his bones and placed them in a shrine.

A manuscript from the time reveals how greatly the Christian community there revered his remains: "We took up his bones, which are more valuable than precious stones and finer than refined gold and laid them in a suitable place, where the Lord will permit us to gather ourselves together, as we are able, in gladness and joy, and to celebrate the birthday of his martyrdom."

Relics, and the shrines where they were kept, were to play an increasingly significant role in Christian healing for centuries to come.

The word "shrine" is based on *scrinium*, a Latin word used to describe a special kind of box which contained important manuscripts. Early Latin-speaking Christians used the same word to describe the container in which the relics of a martyr were kept. Typically, these relics were bones or other parts of the body; but relics might also include objects worn or used by a person venerated as a saint. Ordinarily, shrines were placed in vaults beneath altars. This practice derived from an earlier custom of building churches directly over the tombs of the saints.

Today, the word "shrine" has a broader meaning, that is, as a place where Catholics gather for a particular devotion. Shrines have been established to commemorate Marian apparitions or to house icons instead of relics. The tradition of praying for healing at shrines has continued to the present day. In fact, the most widely accepted and most popular manifestations of healing in the Catholic Church in modern times are the thousands of cures reported at the grotto of Lourdes, France, visited by millions of pilgrims since apparitions of the Blessed Virgin Mary were reported there in 1858. Several dozens of these healings have been investigated by medical authorities and authenticated by the Church as miraculous.

Just as Catholics of the early twentieth century were more likely to seek healing at Lourdes than through the prayers of living Catholic healers, the Catholics of the fourth century were more likely to seek healing through the bones of martyrs.

The veneration of relics is older than Christianity and probably entered the Church through Greek influence. It was a practice common to many religions. The

Jews rejected the practice, but even within the Old Testament there is at least one reference to God's healing power being transmitted through the remains of a holy person. The Second Book of Kings (13:21) relates the story of a dead man being brought back to life after his corpse was hurriedly cast into a grave where Elisha the prophet and miracle worker was buried. Upon coming in contact with Elisha's bones, the dead man was restored to life.

But even if the Jews believed in the power of Elisha's bones, they were prohibited from the veneration of relics. Their law declared that those who touched a human corpse, human bones, or a human grave would remain unclean for seven days.

It is possible that in the earliest days of the Church, when Christianity was still a Jewish sect, the apostles and their followers did not venerate the bones or other bodily relics of saints and martyrs. But, having abandoned the Jewish concept of clean and unclean, they had no reason to prohibit the veneration of relics. They believed that Jesus, not the law, was the means of their salvation. The New Testament does not provide any evidence of the veneration of bodily relics, but the veneration of nonbodily relics is another matter. As we have already seen, early Christians valued handkerchiefs and cloths which had been in contact with Saint Paul's skin, and used them as instruments for healing (see Acts 19:12).

At any rate, the veneration of both bodily and nonbodily relics had become well established in the Church by the middle of the fourth century. The "translation of relics" — moving them from one place to another — began in the Eastern Church in the time of Constantine. In 356 and 357, relics believed to be those of Saints Timothy and Andrew were placed, amid great ceremony, in the Basilica of the Apostles in Constantinople.

Such practices were stronger in the Eastern Church than in the West. In the East, the bodies of saints were dismembered so that a saint's relics could be distributed to various churches. In the West, the Church set severe penalties for desecrating graves, but the code wasn't always obeyed. In fact, it continued for centuries, sometimes with the approval of high Church authorities.

Back in the fourth century, the veneration of relics was so widespread that it created an unhealthy and detestable market for persons who traded in the remains of saints and martyrs. This practice eventually reached the point where the great Saint Augustine (354-430), bishop of Hippo, denounced imposters who dressed up like monks and sold *fake* relics. Eventually, the sale of relics was prohibited by the Church. To this day, the Church prohibits the buying or selling of relics, and local bishops have the authority to excommunicate persons who knowingly sell or distribute false relics or who display them for public veneration.

Although it prohibited the sale of relics, the Church didn't prohibit veneration of them. Many of the Church Fathers — including Saint Jerome, Saint Gregory of Nyssa, and Saint John Chrysostom — took the veneration of relics for granted; some, including Saint Augustine, Saint Ambrose, and Pope Leo I, attributed miraculous cures to such practices.

Many Catholics shared a popular belief that the relics themselves were the source of healing power, but this was never the official teaching of the Church. The scholarly fourth-century theologian Saint Jerome took pains to dissociate the honor given to relics from pagan idolatry: "We do not worship, we do not adore, for fear that we should bow down to the creature rather than to the creator, but we venerate the relics of the martyrs in order the better to adore him whose martyrs they are."

Numerous writings attest that healing did, indeed, occur at medieval shrines. Saint Gregory, bishop of Tours, who was bishop from 573 to 594 in the same diocese where Saint Martin had acquired his reputation as a healer, has written of his own healing at the tomb of Martin. He tells how he was carried, critically ill, to Martin's tomb where he was restored to health. He also tells of healings that resulted when people were anointed with oil from the various shrines of Martin and of the cures of pilgrims who slept in the shrines of saints and martyrs.

Belief in miraculous healings was not universally shared by the Fathers of the Church. Saint Augustine, regarded by the Church as one of the greatest theologians of any era, warned Christians in his early writings not to expect the kind of miraculous healings that had occurred during the age of the apostles. But before the end of his priestly career he had personally witnessed and written about a number of miraculous cures. Reversing his earlier position, he wrote in *The City of God*: "It is a simple fact, then, that there is no lack of miracles even in our day. And the God who works the miracles we read of in the Scripture uses any means and manner He chooses."

At least two of the cures he witnessed occurred in his own church, where relics of the martyr Saint Stephen had been placed. A young man named Paul and his sister, Palladia, both of whom suffered from convulsions, had been coming to the church daily to pray before the martyr's shrine, asking God to forgive their sins and bring them back to health.

On an Easter Sunday, with the church filled, the young man was praying. Augustine gives this account of what happened next: "There at the shrine, grasping the bars of the latticework around the reliquary, stood the young man, praying. Of a sudden he fell prostrate and lay there as if in a trance. However, the convulsions, that ordinarily continued even in his sleep, stopped. The crowd around him were filled with awe and fear. Many wept. Some wanted to lift him to his feet, but others prevented this, thinking it better to wait for him to die. Just as suddenly, he arose. The trembling had stopped. He was cured. There he stood, perfectly normal, looking at the crowd who kept gazing at him. Then everyone burst into a prayer of thankfulness to God. The whole church soon rang with the clamor of rejoicing."

Augustine's description of the scene in the cathedral — again taken from *The City of God* — is remarkably like that of an exuberant charismatic prayer meeting: "In the crowded church, cries of joy rose up everywhere: 'Thanks be to God.' 'Praise be to God.' No tongue was silent. When I held up my hand in salutation, the cries broke out afresh, louder than ever. Only when silence was finally restored could the Scriptural selections appointed for Easter be read."

Augustine tells how, three days after Easter, he asked Paul and Palladia to stand in front of the congregation. As a full account of the young man's healing was read, they stood there in full view of everyone. There was the brother, perfectly calm and fully healed while standing next to him his sister still shook with convulsions. At the end of the reading, the bishop dismissed them and began to speak about the cure. He was still speaking when new cries of rejoicing broke out from the vicinity of the shrine. During the bishop's remarks, Palladia had gone there to pray and, like her brother, had collapsed and risen up cured.

" 'Praise to God' was shouted so loud that my ears could scarcely stand the din," Augustine continues. "But, of course, the main point was that, in the heart of all this clamoring crowd, there burned that faith in Christ for which the martyr Stephen shed his blood."

Augustine not only became firmly convinced of the reality of miracles in his own time, but eventually exercised the gift of healing himself. His biographer, Possidius, in the *Life of St. Augustine*, says that while Augustine was writing *The City of God*, he had been asked to lay hands on a sick man and pray for healing. The result was that the man was cured. But reports of this kind of healing — through the hands and prayers of living Christians — were rare in Augustine's time.

This does not mean that Christians no longer prayed over other Christians for healing. There may have been many such healings that simply went unreported. Also, there may be more truth than we suspect in some of the medieval legends about miracle-working saints.

There is strong evidence that at least until the tenth century, the sacrament of anointing the sick continued to be used with the expectation that healing would occur.

Like the veneration of relics, the practice of anointing the sick was well established in pre-Christian times among the people of the ancient Middle East where oil was used for many purposes, including the treatment of wounds. Anointing of the sick first appears in Christian tradition in the sixth chapter of the Gospel of Mark in which Jesus sends the twelve apostles into the countryside in pairs to preach and to heal. In Mark's words, "They expelled many demons, anointed the sick with oil, and worked many cures" (6:13).

Sacramental anointing in the Catholic Church, as we have already seen, is based on that passage and the Epistle of James (5:13-15) in which the author urges the presbyters, or elders, of the Church to pray over sick individuals, anointing them with oil in the name of the Lord: "This prayer uttered in faith will reclaim the one who is ill, and the Lord will restore him to health."

In the early Church, it was ordinarily the bishops who administered this healing sacrament. But as we have already seen, bishops were not the only Christians who healed. Even in the rite of anointing, oil which had been blessed by a bishop was often applied by lay persons to themselves or to others, with prayers for healing.

In the fifth century, Pope Saint Innocent I wrote to one of his bishops that when Christians were sick, they not only had a right to be anointed by the clergy with holy oil but to "use it themselves for anointing in their own need, or the need of members of their households."

Sacramental anointing of the sick — with the intent to heal — appears to have remained a constant tradition for the first eight hundred years of the Church. But in the tenth century the use of this sacrament took a different turn: instead of being used by Christians generally to restore people to health, it came to be used exclusively by priests to prepare people for death.

This change reflected a shift of attitudes in the Church toward sickness and healing. During the Middle Ages, the Church began placing much greater emphasis on the value of the soul than the worth of the body. Illness and bodily pain were increasingly seen as discipline given to Christians by God for their spiritual strengthening.

Ever since Christianity's acceptance as the official religion of the Roman Empire, there had been a dwindling of the fervor that had been the common tradition of Christians under the Roman persecution. During the Middle Ages, intense devotion and prayer were no longer the way of life of all Christians.

Those who sought a deeper life in Christ entered religious life. Monasteries in the Middle Ages were places of both learning and worship and produced most of the great Christian heroes of the age. Here were the holy men and women who, in the tradition of Saint Anthony, separated themselves from the busy activities of the world and devoted their lives to serving Christ. But even in the monasteries, some Christians were becoming less enthusiastic about healing.

An influential monastic writer of the Middle Ages was a fifth-century monk named John Cassian who wrote a book which discussed, among other things, miraculous gifts. The work, titled *The Conferences*, shows that at least some monastics had begun to be suspicious of attaching too much importance to the gift of healing.

Cassian acknowledged that God did, indeed, bestow the gift of healing on certain "holy and chosen men" for the purposes of healing the sick and building up the faith. But he also wrote that the ability to work miracles was not, of itself, a sign of holiness, and he admonished others that the ability to work miracles carried with it the danger of pride.

"It is better to rid your own heart of the melancholy which corrodes it, than it is to rid someone else of bodily disease," he wrote. "The power which heals your own soul is finer and loftier than the power which heals another's body. The soul is more important than the body, its salvation more urgent."

The Conferences had a strong influence on the thinking and practices of monastic life in the Middle Ages. Saint Benedict, regarded as "The Father of Western Monasticism," considered it one of the books which ought to be read aloud each day by the members of his order.

During the Middle Ages, sick people yearned, as always, for God's healing touch, but it was seen as holier to accept physical sufferings than to ask God to take them away.

Pope Saint Gregory the Great, who reigned from 590 to 604, was apparently the last major writer of the Middle Ages to give personal testimony of having been touched by God's healing power. He writes in his *Dialogues* of many healings, including one in which he himself was cured of a severe illness through the prayers of a monk.

But even though he wrote of healing miracles, Gregory also knew and emphasized the value of suffering. He wrote in his *Book of Pastoral Care*, "The sick are to be admonished that they feel themselves to be sons of God in that the scourge of discipline chastises them."

Those words proved to be more influential in the Church than his testimony about miraculous healings. Three hundred years after the *Book of Pastoral Care* was written, it was still being used in many parts of Europe as a guide to the practice of the Christian faith. The view that God sends sickness to discipline those he loves became strongly implanted in the Church, while the expectation of healing diminished.

The Church had become a more somber place during the Middle Ages. It was a Church more inclined to admonish the sick than to cure them. The poor of medieval Europe, the outcasts, the lepers — the same kind of downtrodden people whom Jesus had loved and healed — had no one to console them. But as the world moved into the thirteenth century, God was raising up a saint who would once again reveal to them the healing power of Christ.

5

The Healer of Assisi

The best known and best loved of all Christian healers was a man who passionately embraced suffering in his own life while he alleviated it in the lives of others.

Giovanni di Bernardone, the man the world would later know and love as Saint Francis, was born in 1182 in the Italian city of Assisi. (One story relates that although he was baptized Giovanni, he was nicknamed Francesco — "the Frenchman" — because his father was away on business in France at the time Francis was born.) Saint Francis is not remembered primarily as a healer, yet his desire and ability to care for the sick and to heal them is closely interwoven with the rest of his life.

No saint who preceded him and no saint who has come after has made a greater impression on the world's people. In many parts of the world, cities, towns, mountains, and rivers bear his name. The way of religious life that he founded is followed today not only by Catholic

Franciscans but by Anglican, Episcopalian, and Lutheran Franciscans as well.

More books have been written about him than any other saint. He is even the hero of a best-selling comic book, published in 1982 by the Marvel Comics Group in cooperation with the religious order that Saint Francis founded.

What sort of man was this little healer of Assisi?

Thomas of Celano, who wrote the first biography of Francis soon after the saint's death, said he was "of medium height, closer to shortness; his head was moderate in size and round, his face a bit long and prominent, his forehead smooth and low; his eyes were of moderate size, black and sound; his hair was black, his eyebrows straight, his nose symmetrical, thin and straight; his ears were upright, but small; his temples smooth."

The biographer goes on to tell us that Francis' "speech was peaceable, fiery and sharp; his voice was strong, sweet, clear and sonorous. His teeth were set close together, even and white; his lips were small and thin; his beard black, but not bushy. His neck was slender, his shoulders straight, his arms short, his hands slender, his fingers long, his nails extended; his legs were thin, his feet small."

Besides this rather pleasing physical description, Francis had an extraordinary desire to live as Jesus had lived. That desire, however, didn't surface until Francis was in his twenties.

Francis came to manhood during the reign of Pope Innocent III. The Church in that era had been involved for centuries in bitter and sometimes bloody struggles for political power. All too often, kings and emperors overruled the pope in Church affairs, and all too often, ill-trained bishops devoted themselves more energetically to amassing wealth than to saving souls.

It was a time of political struggle in Italy as well as elsewhere. During a civil war, the citizens of Assisi had driven out a group of noblemen who had ruled them. The ousted rulers had settled in the nearby rival city of Perugia, while Assisi became a small republic loyal to the pope.

Francis, the son of a wealthy cloth merchant, was fond of good times. He loved to sing and entertain and he threw himself into partying with all the passion and fervor that he would later bring to serving Christ. Everything he did, he did in a grand manner. Although his father was a tradesman, not a nobleman, he had become rich, and the high-spirited Francis gained popularity among Assisi's young noblemen by using his father's money to throw lavish parties.

By 1202, when Francis was twenty, Assisi was on the brink of a new war against Perugia and the ousted rulers who had moved there. When war finally broke out, Francis eagerly went off to fight, dreaming that through his exploits on the battlefield he would become a knight and win a place among Assisi's nobility. But at the battle of Collestrada, Assisi was defeated. The death and destruction that Francis saw were nothing like the glory he had imagined. Even worse, he was captured and sent to a Perugian prison where he remained for a year, sick and disillusioned, until his father was able to ransom him and bring him home.

At home, he became seriously ill and was bedridden for months. After he had recovered, he sought to join a new military expedition being organized by one of Assisi's noblemen. Again, his visions of glory were stirred and once more he set out for battle. But this time his plans were interrupted by a strange prophetic dream in which he saw himself as the leader of a large army of knights. The next night he was awakened from his sleep by what he believed to be the voice of God, calling him to leave the army, abandon his quest for worldly glory, and return to Assisi where he was to seek the Lord's will.

He became a prayerful young man whose interest in parties and rich living had vanished. He was absorbed in the beauty of God's created world and developed a special concern for the poor and sick — particularly lepers, whom he had previously loathed, as mentioned in his writings: "During my life of sin, nothing disgusted me like seeing victims of leprosy. It was the Lord Himself who urged me to go to them. I did so, and ever since, everything was so changed for me that what had seemed at first painful and impossible to overcome became easy and pleasant."

His new behavior puzzled his neighbors and infuriated his father, who tried, without much success, to make Francis work in the family business.

One day, while Francis was praying before a painted wooden crucifix in the broken-down chapel of San Damiano, just outside the city, Christ spoke to him again, calling him by name: "Francis, go repair my house, which is falling in ruins." The young man at first understood it to be a command to repair the ruined chapel where he was praying. He rushed home, helped himself to some of his father's fabrics, and sold them to raise money for the necessary repairs.

His enraged father beat him and brought him before the bishop of Assisi, who told Francis he must give back what he had taken from his father.

"Gladly," said Francis, "and I will do even more." He undressed and gave back to Pietro Bernardone even the clothes he had been wearing. "From now on," he added, "I can advance naked before the Lord saying no longer 'My father, Pietro Bernardone,' but 'Our Father, who art in heaven.'"

The next day, wearing a ragged little coat given him by the bishop's gardener and singing as he walked, he began a new life devoted to living the Gospel in poverty.

One of the first things he did was to immerse himself in the ministry of healing. He went to Gubbio, about twenty miles north of Assisi, where he begged food from an old friend and then went to stay awhile among a group of nearby lepers. The healing that he practiced there was the ordinary kind: the bathing of sores, the removal of encrusted pus. It was miraculous only in the sense that Christ's healing touch had begun to reach these despised outcasts through the gentle hands of a former playboy.

When the rich young man, now a joyful beggar, returned to Assisi to beg food for his body and stones for the reconstruction of San Damiano, many townspeople laughed at him and considered him mad. But there was something about his simplicity, his joy, and his utter lack of pretension that charmed them.

After repairing San Damiano, he began rebuilding some other dilapidated churches, including the Portiuncula, a chapel built in ancient times but by then deserted. Francis loved the Portiuncula and it was here, at a Mass in the restored church, that the nature of his vocation was revealed to him.

According to Thomas of Celano, the gospel text that day told how Christ sent his disciples out to preach and to heal in the surrounding towns and villages: "As you go, make this announcement, 'The reign of God is at hand!' Cure the sick, raise the dead, heal the leprous, expel demons. The gift you have received give as a gift. Provide yourselves with neither gold nor silver nor copper in your belts; no traveling bag, no change of shirt, no sandals, no walking staff. . . ."

The Gospel came alive for Francis, who cried, "This is what I wish, this is what I seek, this is what I long to do with all my heart."

It wasn't long before people stopped laughing and began to recognize that here was a man who found joy and peace in simply following the example and teachings of the Lord Jesus. It wasn't a new teaching that Francis offered, but a simple demonstration that he had accepted Christ's life as his own.

Soon there were others. Bernard of Quintavalle and then Peter of Cattaneo, two of the more prosperous and prominent young men of Assisi, were the first to come, giving away all their money and possessions so that they too might embrace Dame Poverty. Within a few months, there were twelve in all. Francis' vision of himself as the leader of a large army of knights was beginning to be fulfilled, but it was an army that ministered life, not death.

In 1209, Francis and his companions, barefoot and wearing the ragged habits of hermits, walked barefoot to Rome to seek an audience with Pope Innocent III. They were seeking the pope's approval of their new brotherhood as a religious order. The pope, a man better known for his political skills than his Christian charity, didn't really want to be bothered. He suspected this ragged group of young men to be no more than a band of unorthodox reformers or rebels seeking his endorsement for their own purposes. But eventually, Francis' humility and eloquence won Innocent's verbal approval of their proposed rule.

The Order of Friars Minor, as the brothers called themselves, continued to grow. There were thousands of them, even while Francis was still alive. They loved poverty, they loved prayerful solitude, and, most of all, they loved taking care of the despised lepers whom Francis called, "my Christian brothers." Francis strove to love these unfortunate people as Christ himself loved them. And as he strove, marvelous things began to occur.

"And so it happened many times," we are told in the *Fioretti (The Little Flowers of Saint Francis)*, "that God by His power simultaneously healed the soul of one whose body the Saint healed, as we read of Christ."

As an example, the *Fioretti*, written about a hundred years after the death of Francis, relates this story:

In a certain hospital where the friars had been working, there was a victim of leprosy who constantly attacked any of the friars who tried to help him. He not only insulted them but blasphemed Jesus and his Mother so terribly that none of the friars would go near him.

The friars told Francis, who went to the man himself, greeting him with the friars' customary salutation, "God give you peace, my dear brother."

"What peace can I have from God, who has taken from me all peace and everything that is good, and has made me all rotten and stinking?" the man asked.

"My dear son," Francis replied, "be patient, because the weaknesses of the body are given to us in this world by God for the salvation of the soul. So they are of great merit when they are borne patiently."

"How can I bear patiently this constant pain that is afflicting me day and night? For not only am I burned and crucified by my sickness, but I am sorely wronged by the friars whom you gave me to take care of me, because there is not one who serves me the way he should."

So Francis himself agreed to take care of the man, telling him, "I will do whatever you want."

"I want you to wash me all over, because I smell so bad that I cannot stand it myself," the man said.

So while one of the friars poured water over the patient, Francis washed him. And, according to the *Fioretti*, "wherever Saint Francis touched him with his holy hands, the leprosy disappeared, and the flesh remained completely healed."

Yet it was not only the man's body that had been healed. Overcome by the humility and gentleness Francis had shown him, he wept and repented of his blasphemies and his insults against the friars.

Francis, with characteristic humility, left the region in order to avoid any worldly glory that might result from having miraculously healed the man. A few weeks later, the man fell ill with another disease and, after receiving the sacraments of the Church, died what the *Fioretti* calls "a holy death."

The writings of Thomas of Celano, like those in the *Fioretti*, depict Francis as someone who frequently healed the sick through supernatural means.

Thomas, who apparently entered the Order of Friars Minor between 1213 and 1216, was commissioned by Pope Gregory IX to write the *First Life of Francis*. It is not a biography in the sense that we understand that word today. It is not a complete account of the life of Francis, nor did Thomas mean it to be. It was, rather, an account of the marvelous things Francis had done which demonstrated his sanctity. Because of this, Thomas emphasized the spiritual nature of the events he recorded and frequently reported them as being supernatural.

One of the first healings attributed to Francis by Thomas involves a young child, "lame and weak of body," who was the son of a soldier who had given Francis hospitality in the city of Toscanella: "Though he was a young child, he had passed the years of weaning; still he remained in a cradle. When the father of the boy saw the great sanctity of the man of God, he humbly cast himself at his feet, begging from him health for his son. But Francis, who considered himself useless and unworthy of such great power and grace, refused for a long time to do this." Finally yielding to the man's insistent petitions, Francis "prayed and then put his hand upon the boy and, blessing him, raised him up. Immediately, with all present looking on and rejoicing, the boy arose completely restored and began to walk here and there about the house."

Thomas provides many more similar stories. In the diocese of Narni, a man named Peter who has been paralyzed for five months is restored to health when Francis makes the sign of the cross over him. In the same locale, a blind woman's sight is restored when the saint draws the sign of the cross on her eyes.

In the city of Gubbio, Francis is moved to pity when a woman runs to him and begs him to touch her crippled hands. He does so and she is healed. Thomas touchingly adds: "Immediately the woman went home full of joy, made a kind of cheese cake with her own hands, and offered it to the holy man. He took a little of it in his kindness and commanded the woman to eat the rest of it with her family."

Another story written by Thomas tells how a friar was among those that Francis healed: "One of the brothers suffered frequently from a very serious infirmity and one horrible to see; I do not know by what name it is called, though some think it is an evil spirit. Frequently he was cast upon the ground and he turned about foaming at the mouth and with a terrible look upon his face; at times his limbs were drawn up, at other times they were extended; now they were folded up and twisted, again they were rigid and hard. Sometimes, when he was stretched out and rigid, he would be raised up into the air to the height of a man's stature, with his feet even with his head, and then would fall back to the ground. Pitying his grievous illness, the holy father Francis went to him and after praying, signed him and blessed him. Suddenly he was cured and he did not again suffer in the least from the tortures of this illness."

It is possible that certain of the events that Thomas reports as miracles could have occurred naturally. But Thomas, who knew Francis and believed in the miraculous nature of these healings, reported the truth as he saw it. There are some who take Thomas's writings at face value and others who will be suspicious of any such collection of miracle tales.

Nevertheless this does not diminish the value of these stories which consistently depict Francis as a servant of Christ who was able to make people well in body and in spirit. Persons who are familiar with the healing ministry, who have perhaps experienced healing at the hands of a prayerful Christian or group of Christians, will recognize that all true healing, miraculous or otherwise, is an act of God.

Yet Francis, although he healed, is not remembered primarily as a healer. His healings, like those of Peter, Paul, Anthony of the Desert, and Martin of Tours, were a manifestation of his love for others and a sign of the Holy Spirit's presence; but they were only one part of his ministry.

Francis is better known for his extraordinary ability to preach the Gospel, to draw others to Jesus, and to communicate Christ's peace. He is remembered as the founder of one of the world's most vital religious orders, as a man so in tune with God's creation that even birds and animals loved him — a man whose entire life proclaimed the joy of following God.

How, one may ask, was he able to do this? The answer, putting it simply, lies in Francis' imitating Christ so well that people whose faith had grown lukewarm were suddenly jolted by the discovery that Christ's own life was being manifested again in their midst.

He not only preached the virtues Christ preached but also practiced them: wholehearted devotion to God, poverty, humility, gentleness, and tender compassion for the poor, the weak, and the sick. His way of life seemed extreme, even to the Church authorities of his time, but it was simply faithfulness to the Gospel.

Lord Guido, bishop of Assisi, was one of those who tried to persuade Francis to abandon his radical commitment to poverty. "Your way of life appears too hard and impractical," he told the saint.

"My Lord," Francis replied, "if we owned property, we should need arms to defend it. Besides, property engenders many disputes and lawsuits harmful to love of God and neighbor. That is why we do not want to have anything of our own here below."

The bishop, who could not dispute this without also disputing the Gospel, made no further effort to change Francis' mind.

In all things, Francis conscientiously strove to make his life a duplicate of Christ's. He found joy in doing this — such joy that others were drawn to follow him. But in his later years, he increasingly understood that to fully participate in the life of Christ, he must suffer as Jesus did.

Francis suffered as a result of his own poor health, his mortifications of the body, and his severe fasting; but he suffered even more over divisions within the Friars Minor which forced him to accept compromises of his original vision.

It was on the summit of a mountain called La Verna, as Francis knelt in prayer before sunrise, that he felt death approaching and begged God for two things: "to experience in myself in all possible fullness the pains of Your cruel Passion, and to feel for You the same love that made You sacrifice Yourself for us."

As he continued to pray, he saw the crucified Christ in the form of a seraph. The figure descended from heaven and marked Francis with visible, painful signs of Christ's own crucifixion. From that day forward, Francis' body was marked with wounds in his hands, feet, and side.

In Francis' time, as in ours, the Church taught that the acceptance of suffering is a path to grace. By accepting suffering, those who follow Christ can experience healing of the soul if not the body. That view of suffering has helped many believers to accept their suffering and to use it, as Francis did, to grow closer to Jesus.

That view of suffering, however, doesn't change the fact that God also heals. Jesus accepted suffering, yet he treated disease as if it were an enemy. So did Saint Francis.

6

A Woman's Healing Touch

Most of the well-known healers in the Catholic Church have been men. That is not because God bestows healing gifts less generously among women but because women have had less opportunity than men to engage in public ministry.

It is possible that the Church has had just as many female as male healers; but, until the last few centuries, their gifts were seldom exercised in public. No one has ever counted the women whose quiet faith and loving prayers have restored the health and spirit of ailing children, friends, and fellow believers.

Nevertheless, in the middle of the fourteenth century — more than one hundred twenty years after the death of Francis of Assisi — a woman was born in Italy who did things no woman had ever done before.

Catherine of Siena was a mystic, a healer, a preacher, a lover of the poor, a peacemaker, and a papal diplomat. She was canonized by Pope Pius II in 1461 and was declared a Doctor of the Church in 1970 by Pope Paul VI in recognition of her writings, particularly *The Dialogue of Saint Catherine of Siena.*

She was, above all, a woman who loved our Lord. The world knows Catherine for her ecstasies and for her remarkable role as a diplomat and adviser to popes. The ecstasies, however, weren't just a peculiar trait of a saintly mystic. They were an expression of her intimate relationship with her divine Savior. When he spoke to her, she forgot everything else.

It was her intense spiritual relationship with Jesus that produced not only her ecstasies but her ability to do extraordinary things for the One she loved. Advising popes was just one of them. No less remarkable were the ways in which she ministered peace and healing to some of the poorest and most wretched people of the fourteenth century.

She was born in 1347 at Fontebranda in Siena on March 25, the feast of the Annunciation, which that year fell on Palm Sunday. Catherine and a twin sister were the last of twenty-five children born to a wealthy dyer, Giacomo Benincasa, and his wife, Lapa di Piagenti di Puccio. Catherine's twin sister, Giovanna, died in infancy, and few of the other Benincasa children lived to adulthood.

Her father was a quiet, sensitive, and deeply spiritual man. Her mother was hard-working, energetic, and honest, but sharp-tongued and neither as patient nor as bright as her husband.

The Benincasa home was on a hill on the Via dei Tintori just below the Dominican monastery at Camporeggi. As a small child, Catherine was fascinated by, and attracted to, the friars who often came through the street in their white habits with black mantles.

When she was only six, she had an experience that turned her life in a direction different from the ways of other children. It happened one evening while she and her brother Stephen were returning from an errand. As the children descended a steep lane with steps, Catherine began gazing across a little valley where the evening sun was turning the clouds to gold above the familiar bell tower of the old church of Saint Dominic.

While Stephen continued walking, Catherine saw in the sky a vision of Jesus, clothed in glorious robes. As she continued to gaze, Jesus looked toward her, smiled, then extended his hand to bless her.

Stephen had reached the bottom of the hill before he discovered that his younger sister was no longer with him. He turned and called to her, but she didn't answer. He ran back up the hill and grabbed her hand. Coming out of her trancelike state, she described the vision to her brother, then began to weep because the vision was gone.

After that, little Catherine spent many hours listening to stories of martyrs and hermits and playing games in which she would imitate them. Inspired by what she had heard of the desert Fathers, she sometimes set out alone imagining that somewhere on the outskirts of Siena she would find a desert in which to meditate. Once she did find a small cave under a shelving rock in the hills near her home and spent the rest of the day praying there.

It must have been difficult for Catherine's parents to tell whether she was playing or praying, but for Catherine, such distinctions didn't exist. Her greatest joy in playing "hermit" was that in her playful prayers, God was speaking to her.

The Dominican who later became her spiritual director and biographer, Raymond of Capua, reports miracles that were popularly attributed to her childhood; but those who knew her best, her parents, apparently did not see Catherine as a child of exceptional sanctity. Thus, it seems plausible that some of these stories were invented by others after Catherine became famous.

It was not until she was twelve that her parents began to realize that their daughter's piety was more than ordinary child's play. She was approaching what was then a marriageable age, and her mother and father began to consider what sort of marriage might be arranged for her. But Catherine would hear none of it.

Her parents didn't know it, but five years earlier, when she was only seven, Catherine had prayed before an image of Our Lady, promising she would never have any bridegroom except Jesus. Raymond has attributed these words to her: "Most blessed and most holy Virgin, look not upon my weakness, but grant me the grace that I may have for my bridegroom Him whom I love with all my soul, thy most holy Son, our only Lord, Jesus Christ! I promise Him and thee that never will I have any other bridegroom."

Despite Catherine's protests, her mother tirelessly sought to persuade her to dress and adorn herself in ways that would attract suitors. Catherine never wavered in her nuptial vows to Mary and Jesus, but on one occasion she yielded to her mother's efforts to make her more attractive to men. She dressed up as her parents wanted her to, and immediately regretted it. For the rest of her life, she expressed horror at having yielded to such a worldly temptation. Determined to resist her parents' plans for her marriage, she shaved her head, an act by which Religious women in Catherine's day renounced attractiveness to men.

Eventually, her parents gave in. Her father is said to have told her, "May God preserve us, dearest daughter, from trying in any way to set up ourselves against the will of God. We have long seen that it was no childish whim of thine, and now we know clearly that it is the spirit of God that constrains thee. Keep thy vow therefore, and live as the Spirit tells thee; we will no longer hinder thee. We ask thee only for one thing, always to intercede for us in prayer, so that we may be worthy of the promises of thy Bridegroom."

In a touching display of parental sensitivity he told the rest of the family, "Let no one dare in any way to torment or hinder my dear daughter. She is to be left free and in peace to serve her Bridegroom and continually to pray for us. We could never get a bridegroom of mightier kindred."

Catherine spent most of her teen years in seclusion in a cell set aside for her in her parents' house. The room, which she rarely left except to go to Mass, became her "desert" where she — like Anthony — fasted, prayed, fought spiritual battles, and conversed with Jesus. She treated her body harshly, wearing a hair shirt and sleeping as little as an hour a day — on a board instead of a bed. She fasted practically to the point of starvation, and eventually her only food was the Eucharist. Her mother, still not reconciled to Catherine's austere spiritual practices, insisted that she eat more. Catherine would sometimes try to oblige, but the extra food made her sick.

When she was about sixteen, Catherine joined the Mantellate, an order of Dominican women tertiaries who wore habits and made traditional vows of poverty, chastity, and obedience but who lived at home, as Catherine did, instead of in convents.

The Mantellate were older women, mostly widows, who at first refused to accept someone as young as Catherine. They relented only after the prioress had visited the Benincasa home to make sure that Catherine wasn't "too pretty."

None of Catherine's biographers has described her as beautiful. "Nature had not given her a face over-fair," Raymond admits in her biography. Her features were not well proportioned, but her face was so bright and vivacious that people found her delightful.

In the solitude of her room she continued to pray, but diabolical apparitions appeared, tempting and tormenting her. They ridiculed her decision to abandon the joys and pleasures of the material world. But as she prayed and constantly sought refuge in Jesus, she gradually became more aware, more certain of Christ's presence, and the conflicts began to subside.

The years that followed brought great peace and joy and an even deeper intimacy with the Lord. In her desire to read the Old Testament psalms and the Gospel, she taught herself to read. She learned so quickly that it was commonly said that she had been miraculously taught by an angel.

During this period, Christ appeared to her in a vision, holding a ring in which was set a beautiful, flawless diamond. As he placed the ring on her finger, she heard the words, "I, thy Creator and Redeemer, espouse thee in faith and love. . . . Perform with a dauntless spirit the works which my providence will assign to thee; thou shalt triumph over all enemies."

Gradually, to her discomfort, she heard Christ calling her to give up the solitude which she had grown to love and to begin ministering to others.

"I am but a woman, and I am ignorant," she argued. "What can I do?"

"In my sight, there is not man nor woman, not learned nor unlearned," she heard the Lord reply. "But know that in these last times the pride of the so-called learned and wise has risen to such heights that I have resolved to humble them. I will therefore send unlearned men, full of divine wisdom, and women who will put to shame the learning that men think they have. And I have resolved to send thee also out into the world, and wheresoever thou shalt go I will be with thee and never leave thee, and I will guide thee in all that thou must do."

Catherine's reservations were well founded. The customs and social practices of Europe in the Middle Ages had left young women with only two options: marriage or the cloister. When she ended her seclusion, she began taking care of her family's needs, happily doing the most menial chores. Only gradually did she begin ministering to persons outside her family's house. She began by comforting and giving alms to the poor families who lived nearby. She had a remarkable gift for peacemaking which she used in settling disputes and feuds between families — constant internecine fighting being one of the unfortunate characteristics of Sienese life at that time.

As she began to move into public life, the Mantellate watched with growing apprehension because it was unprecedented and contrary to all custom for an unmarried girl to act in such a manner. Catherine became the center of controversy and, for a time, scandal. Some of the Mantellate felt threatened and perhaps a bit jealous to see such freedom and holiness in one so young.

At one point, some of the older sisters formed a committee to investigate rumors that Catherine was sexually immoral. Catherine insisted that she was a virgin, but beyond that she didn't take the committee very seriously and continued her public ministry.

But if some were scandalized, others were charmed and amazed by the ways in which Catherine brought Christ's gentle and healing touch to those around her. One of her modern biographers, Margaret Roberts, has observed that during the early days of her public ministry "her voice, lovely both in speech and song, soothed [the] dying. . . ; her touch and prayers healed the sick; it was told that the daughter of Giacomo Benincasa cured when the doctor had said there was no hope, and with each sufferer restored to health her fame grew."

Among those she healed was her mother who, near death, refused to see a priest but told Catherine, "As you are so holy, as they are always telling me, then go and pray to Our Lord that I may get well." Catherine prayed, but Lapa grew worse and finally stopped breathing. Yet Catherine continued to pray and her mother was not only restored to life but outlived many of her children and grandchildren, including Catherine.

Eventually, Catherine's reputation was so great that Pope Gregory XI sent a letter to her granting her permission (although she had not requested it) to travel about the countryside, preaching and healing. She was to be accompanied by three friars who would hear confessions.

In Catherine, the gift of healing was intertwined with her compassion for the sick, the poor, and those in prison. This quality of tender mercy was not much in vogue among her contemporaries. The mid-fourteenth century was not an age of compassion, but Catherine knew she had been sent by Christ to serve those whom the rest of the world despised.

She seemed even more concerned with conversion of hearts than with healing. She frequently visited condemned felons, helping them prepare for their executions. The best known of these visits was to a young man named Niccolo di Toldo, whose crime had been to make some derogatory remarks against the government. Outraged that he was to be executed for such a trivial offense, he sent word to Catherine, begging her to visit him.

Her visit encouraged the young man. He accepted

his fate, went to confession, and told Catherine that if she would attend his execution, he would die gladly.

The next day, Catherine arrived early at the place of execution. She later told Raymond in a letter, "Before he came I laid my own neck on the block. . . . Over it I prayed, and said, 'Mary!' for I wanted to obtain the grace that at this moment light and peace might enter his heart, and then I saw him coming. My soul was so filled that though there was a great crowd I saw no one. . . . And he came like a meek lamb, and seeing me he began to smile, and bade me sign the cross over him, and then I said, 'To the bridal feast, gentle brother; soon you will attain eternal life.' "

When the time came, Catherine tenderly held Niccolo's head and arranged it for the executioner's ax. His head fell into her hands and his blood spattered Catherine who, praying with her eyes closed, saw a vision of the young man's soul entering the open wound in Christ's side.

Just as she visited prisons, she spent much time at hospitals and among the lepers. Like Saint Francis, she did whatever she could to comfort the sick and to share with them the good news of salvation. Sometimes this meant nursing them; sometimes it meant curing them through prayer.

There was nothing in her healings that smacked of superstition. She just matter-of-factly expected God to make certain people well.

In 1374, Siena lay in the grip of "the black death," bubonic plague, which took the life of one out of every three Europeans. While the epidemic was raging, Catherine, accompanied by Raymond and two other friars, worked almost without rest tending the sick and burying the dead. She walked from hospital to hospital and to the houses of the poor.

At the Casa della Misericordia hospital, the rector, a man named Matteo, lay dying. The physician attending him told Raymond there was no hope. In deep sorrow, the friar left Matteo's bedside and went to minister to others.

Later that day, Catherine heard the sad news and hastened to Matteo's room. Even as she approached, Matteo could hear her bright, energetic voice in the corridor gently admonishing him to get out of bed. Matteo, encouraged by her cheerful manner, smiled and found the strength to get to his feet.

Not long after, the grieving Raymond chanced to meet Catherine and said, "Will you let one so dear to me, so useful to others, die?"

She replied, "Am I like God to deliver a man from death?"

But Raymond insisted, "I know that you obtain from God whatever you will."

Catherine stood with her head bent, then smiled a little. Looking Raymond directly in the eye, she said, "Courage, he will not die this time." As Catherine walked away, Raymond hurried back to the director's bedside where he found Matteo risen and exclaiming, "Do you know what she has done for me?"

The other friars, Fra Bartolomeo di Dominici and the hermit Fra Santi, also had occasion to witness Catherine's exercise of healing gifts. They told of seeing her standing over the sick "and commanding the fever to leave them. And immediately rising, they went to their work."

Raymond himself tells of becoming ill with fever, headache, and a swelling in the groin, symptoms that matched those of the plague. One of the friars helped Raymond walk to Catherine's house, but because she was not home, he lay down on a bench where Catherine later found him. She knelt by the bench, placed her hand upon his feverish brow, and prayed without words.

As she prayed, he writes, "It was as if something was being pulled out of me at the ends of all my limbs." After half an hour, Catherine stood up and the symptoms were gone.

Catherine gave him something to eat and, after he had rested a bit, told him, "Go out again for the salvation of souls and give thanks to the Highest Who has saved you."

Not every sick person whom she encountered was healed. And more than once, the persons that she nursed treated her with contempt. An elderly woman named Tecca, suffering from leprosy, was one of these. Not only were her leprous wounds repulsive, but she spoke evil of all who came near her. No one wanted to have anything to do with her.

Despite the woman's unruly manner, Catherine "saw her Bridegroom in that leper and therefore she served her diligently and with reverence," Raymond writes. Tecca responded by verbally abusing Catherine. Yet Catherine continued to serve the woman even though others told her she risked contracting leprosy herself. Eventually, suspicious-looking eruptions appeared on Catherine's hands, but still she ministered to Tecca as if she were nursing Christ himself. When Tecca died, Catherine washed the body and buried it with her own hands. It is said that on the day of Tecca's burial, the skin of Catherine's hands became clean once more.

Catherine's role as healer was closely linked with her role as a peacemaker and was no less extraordinary. From the very beginning of her public ministry, she exhibited a remarkable ability to heal broken relationships as well as sick bodies. Often, she was able to settle violent disputes between workers and their employers or between feuding families.

In 1374, in the midst of the plague, a particularly vicious feud was raging between three important Sienese families. Catherine was called in as a mediator. She appointed a day for the families to meet in the Church of San Cristofero, but at the appointed time, only one of the factions met Catherine there. The other two families had decided not to seek peace. "They will not listen to me," she observed. "Very well, they will listen to God."

She remained in the church praying. Eventually, the other two families arrived, not ready to seek peace but to ridicule their enemies. Yet when they saw and heard Catherine praying for them, they were so moved and touched that they became ashamed and held out their hands to their enemies.

It was her ability as a peacemaker that led her into politics — a path seldom traveled by other mystics and contemplatives. At that time, the papacy was in exile in Avignon, France. Italy was divided into many autonomous city-states, and civil wars were more or less continuous among them.

Catherine was distressed by division and schism in the Church. She embraced the vision of a united Italy, loyal to the pope, and — despite ill health — worked energetically, using all her powers of persuasion, to reunite disaffected factions.

Eventually, Pope Gregory XI sent her on a successful diplomatic mission to Pisa, and in 1370, when Florence rose openly against the authority of the pope, Catherine was chosen as a mediator, an extraordinary role for any woman, especially a contemplative healer and mystic.

In Florence she won the trust of the Guelphs (the papal popular party) as well as that of the Ghibellines (the imperial aristocratic party). Both parties authorized her to begin peace negotiations with the pope at Avignon.

When Catherine arrived at Avignon, the cardinals didn't welcome her presence. She preached a return of the papacy to Rome, a move which would inevitably involve shifts of power within the Church. These high churchmen questioned the spirituality and intellectual capacity of this audacious woman and insisted on testing her. Many of them tried to trick her, but her straightforward manners and innocent good sense eventually won the respect of most of them.

At Avignon, she is credited with having persuaded Pope Gregory XI to return the papacy to Rome, ending its exile of nearly seventy years.

Her influential position in the Church did not, however, put an end to her ministry of healing. As she and her companions were returning to Italy from Avignon, they stopped at an inn in Toulon where a woman with a sick baby insisted that Catherine be called from her room to cure the child. "She has the power with God, and can heal diseases," the mother said. "She can restore to me my baby who is dying."

Catherine dreaded being made the center of attention, but the mother's sobs aroused her compassion. She came out of her room, took the child in her arms, and prayed. The child immediately began to improve and the whole city was aware of what had happened.

Pope Gregory died in 1378 and was succeeded by Urban VI, but many in the Church sought to return the papacy to Avignon and hated the new pope. Urban's enemies declared his election illegal and elected another pope who was installed as Clement VII at Avignon. That left the Church with two popes, both claiming supreme authority. Catherine remained loyal to Pope Urban who continued to use her diplomatic skills as Pope Gregory had.

In her distress over the difficulties afflicting the Church, she offered herself as a victim to God. By this time in her life she, like Saint Francis, had been marked with the stigmata — the visible signs of Christ's suffering on the cross. When the wounds had first appeared on Catherine's hands, she had feared that they would unnecessarily draw attention to her and she begged God to keep them invisible. After that, the wounds, although painful, could not be seen by others.

Catherine, who had always insisted that sadness

constituted the worst fault of all in a disciple of Christ, accepted her suffering gladly. She had no desire for anything but death and prayer, as these were her path to union with her beloved Jesus. She died in Rome on April 29, 1380, after a painful illness. She was thirty-three years old. After she died, the stigmata, which she had borne in secret, became visible to all who gazed on her body.

Part
Three

Catholic Healers of the Recent Past

7

The Miracle Man of Montreal

Alfred Bessette was a nobody. He came into the world so sickly and weak that his parents, fearing he would die, baptized him themselves, not daring to wait for the parish priest. He was an orphan at the age of twelve and because of poor health and almost no education, he couldn't hold a job.

He was poor and sickly all his life but managed to live ninety-one years. By the time he died he was so well known and loved that an estimated one million people came to pray beside his coffin. To these people, the man in the coffin wasn't Alfred Bessette, the failure, but Brother André, humble servant of God, whose prayers made people well and restored their faith.

This was not a healer of centuries ago, but a man who lived and healed in our own time and on our own continent.

He was born on August 9, 1845, in the tiny Canadian village of St. Grégoire, about thirty miles southeast of Montreal. Poverty and illiteracy were a way of life for many of the French-speaking families of Iberville County, and the family of Isaac and Clothilde Bessette was no exception.

Alfred was the eighth of twelve children and the sickliest of them all. His father, Isaac, like many of his neighbors, was illiterate, unable to write even his own name. He worked hard as a carpenter and wheelwright, constantly struggling — without much success — to meet his family's needs.

In their poverty, the members of the Bessette family recognized their dependency on God, and little Alfred learned to pray early. Reciting the rosary together was a family custom. During those family prayers, Alfred would reach out to touch his mother's rosary.

"My mother, knowing I was delicate, seemed to show more affection for me than for the other children," he would recall in later years. "While we were saying our family prayers together, I stayed near her and followed the prayers on her beads."

Clothilde, a simple, devout woman, also taught Alfred to love and depend on Mary's husband, Saint Joseph, who worked as a carpenter to take care of his family — just as Alfred's father did until one terrible day when Alfred was ten.

Isaac was cutting timber when a tree fell upon him and crushed him to death, leaving Clothilde alone to raise their large family. The responsibility proved to be more than she could manage. Exhausted, she allowed most of the children to be raised by other families. Only Alfred, the feeblest of her children, remained with her.

She moved with him to St. Césaire d'Iberville to live with her sister Rosalie Nadeau. But two and a half years later, discouraged and broken by her husband's death, Clothilde died.

The boy remained with the Nadeaus at first; but his uncle, Timothy, is said to have been a severe man, and Alfred lived there only long enough to prepare for his first Holy Communion and his confirmation and to learn to sign his name and read a little. Later he was taken in by the mayor of St. Césaire for whom Alfred worked for a time as a farmhand.

The deaths of his parents meant that he would have little schooling. An orphan, without money or education and suffering from chronic ill health, Alfred dropped out of school and, in his early teens, began to seek work in neighboring villages. He worked as an apprentice baker, shoemaker, blacksmith, and tinsmith; but because of his bad health, he failed at each of these trades.

He was a teenager when the Civil War broke out in the United States. Young New England mill workers were marching off to fight in the South, and many Canadians migrated to America lured by jobs in the industrial Northeast. Eighteen-year-old Alfred Bessette was among these Canadian job seekers. He moved to Connecticut in about 1863 and worked mainly in textile mills. After the war, he returned to Canada, living for a time with relatives and then returning to St. Césaire. With his poor health and his lack of education, he was unable to earn an adequate living.

Faced with loneliness and discouragement, the young man's only solace was in prayer — particularly to Saint Joseph. His parish priest, Father André Provençal, befriended him and thought that although Alfred lacked the educational background to become a priest, he might have a vocation as a Religious brother. The priest urged him to apply to the Congregation of Holy Cross which had recently opened a school across the road from the parish church. Following the pastor's advice, Alfred, now twenty-five, knocked at the door of the novitiate of the community. Father Provençal, in a letter to the superiors of the community, wrote, "I am sending you a saint."

Alfred's devotion to Saint Joseph must surely have played a part in his decision. The brothers of Holy Cross at that time were widely known as the Brothers of Saint Joseph. And on December 8, 1870, only sixteen days before Alfred began his novitiate, Pope Pius IX had proclaimed Saint Joseph patron of the universal Church. Those facts were not lost on Alfred, who had learned at an early age to depend on the prayers of the carpenter who raised Jesus.

Alfred probably felt certain that he was moving in the right direction, but the provincial council of the congregation wasn't so sure. Wary of Alfred's poor health, the council decided at first not to allow him to profess religious vows but permitted him to remain with the congregation as a novice. He was assigned to Saint Joseph's Novitiate in Montreal and took "André" as his religious name, after his friend, Father Provençal.

Brother André was given the position of porter at a school for boys, the Collège Notre-Dame, which the congregation operated on Queen Mary Road in the village of

Côte-des-Neiges directly opposite the steep slope of Mount Royal, the mountain for which Montreal is named. The job of porter was a humble one and it was to be his official function for the next four decades. Brother André's duties were to answer the door, keep the lamps filled with oil, and supply the fireplaces with fuel. In later years, with characteristic wit, he would comment, "My superiors showed me to the door, and I stayed there for forty years." He had other chores too, all of them as humble as he was. He washed dishes, mended clothes, gave haircuts, and ran messages.

For two years he lived in the Holy Cross community without knowing whether he would be allowed to profess his vows. During that uncertain period, he had a long talk with Father Narcisse Hupier, an elderly member of the congregation who was visiting Montreal briefly on his way to an assignment in New Brunswick. He impressed on André the importance of welcoming God's will, even when it meant suffering and hardship. It was a lesson that would guide Brother André for the rest of his life, leading him in paths traveled earlier by Saints Francis and Catherine.

His suffering included painful digestive problems as well as the uncertainty of not knowing whether the congregation would continue to let him stay. Because of his bad stomach, his meals were frequently nothing more than bread or flour mixed with milk. The rest of the community knew of his health problems, but they had little opportunity to observe the way he ate. His duties as porter often required him to be "on the door" while the others were taking their meals.

In 1872, he was permitted to profess his first vows. He made his perpetual vows in 1875 at the age of thirty. It was at about that time that people began to attribute extraordinary cures to the prayers and faith of Brother André.

One early incident involved an outbreak of smallpox at another school operated by the congregation in St. Laurent, just north of Montreal. Brother André urged that members of the community carry a statue of Saint Joseph around the affected school while praying for the saint's intercession and protection. This was done and the sickness immediately began to abate.

That incident might have been forgotten except that other healings started to occur in his own community at Collège Notre-Dame. Most of them flowed out of his friendship with the students. He loved being with them, and they enjoyed his company. Often, he took them on long walks. They knew him as a congenial man who enjoyed joking with them, but he commanded their respect too. He had an air of sanctity, sympathy, and faith that impressed those who met him. The students — and visitors too — confided in him easily. His attitude of hope and faith comforted them.

He made it his duty to visit students who fell sick, and always, before he left them, he would pray, asking Saint Joseph to protect them. Sometimes he would tell them to rub themselves with religious medals struck with the image of Saint Joseph. At other times, he would recommend that they be anointed with oil from one of the lamps that burned before a statue of the saint.

It is said that many of them became well instantly, and word of the cures began to spread. Eventually, some of the parents began asking Brother André to pray for cures for their own ailments, and after that, other sick persons who lived in the area heard about his unusual gift and began coming to the school to seek his prayers.

His compassion for the poor and the sick was probably heightened by his own illness and poverty. Many of the poor who came to the school seeking food or other assistance must have reminded him of his own family and other families he had grown up with. He was one of them. They found Brother André a compassionate friend who offered food, encouragement, and consolation as readily as he offered prayer.

In 1878, a member of the community known as Brother Aldéric was suffering from a seriously infected leg wound which had failed to heal after two months of treatment. On Brother André's advice, the brother treated the ailing leg with "Saint Joseph's oil," and prayed to Saint Joseph for a cure. The next morning, the pain was gone, and in two days the wound had completely healed. In that same year, the first written testimony of five cures attributed to Brother André's prayers was published.

As his reputation spread, large numbers of sick people began showing up at the school looking for Brother André. The community wasn't happy about what was happening. Visiting parents sometimes were upset to find school corridors filled with sick people whose illnesses might be contagious. Meanwhile, skeptical members of the medical profession had begun to accuse

Brother André of quackery. It looked as if the entire community might be subjected to ridicule, and some of its members were blaming the brother who was becoming popularly known as the "Miracle Man of Montreal."

As a result, Brother André was forbidden to receive sick visitors. It was easy to control the humble and obedient Brother André, but more difficult to control the poor, who continued to come to the school. When they were told that Brother André was unable to see them, they simply waited in silence. Finally, a compromise was found. Brother André was told he could receive the sick, but not in the school.

On a vacant lot across the road, the religious community had erected a small shelter for people traveling to or from the school by trolley car. Brother André was given permission to see his visitors there. Always he sought not only the healing of physical ailments but also the conversion of hardened hearts. "My greatest pleasure," he once said, "is to reconcile a sinner to God."

The crowds grew. Among them were many lay people who had experienced healing or conversion through the prayers of Brother André. He began to envision a small chapel, or oratory, where these devout lay people could pray in devotion to Saint Joseph. He told Brother Aldéric that he believed Saint Joseph wanted to be honored with the construction of such an oratory on a steep slope of the mountain that rose directly beyond the trolley shelter.

The community didn't own the property but had grown concerned about speculation that a tavern might be built there. The congregation was considering purchasing the land to prevent that from happening. When Brother Aldéric heard Brother André's dreams of building an oratory on Mount Royal, he decided to try, in his own way, to influence the purchase of the property. Quietly, he crossed the road, climbed the steep slope and buried a Saint Joseph's medal on the land. Brother André also began to scatter medals of Saint Joseph on the property. In 1896, the congregation acquired the parcel.

When Brother André first asked his superior for permission to build a chapel, the answer was "no." But soon, the superior agreed to let him build a tiny oratory, using money that Brother André had accumulated over the years as the community's barber. At five cents a haircut, the Miracle Man had raised two hundred dollars.

That amount wouldn't go far. A road had to be built up the steep side of the mountain, and before a chapel could be erected, a level site would have to be prepared. The brother's lay friends took charge of the work and the raising of additional funds.

With the approval of Archbishop Paul Bruchesi of Montreal, the work went forward. As always, Brother André and his friends trusted that God, through the intercession of Saint Joseph, would provide whatever was needed.

Contributions came. Not usually in large amounts, but enough to allow the work to continue. Sometimes, at the end of a week, the workers would ask, "Shall we come back on Monday?" Brother André would have to reply, "I don't know. I don't have any more money." On Monday, the workers would come back and somehow, in the meantime, more money had come.

The road to the property was completed and was dubbed "St. Joseph's Boulevard." The oratory, when it was finished in 1904, was nothing more than a simple wooden chapel which measured only fifteen by eighteen feet. It accommodated an altar and had room for a priest and a few servers. That was all. There was no room left inside for pews. But the back of the chapel was constructed in such a way that it could be opened like two large doors. The faithful sat on pews on the grassy slope of the mountain, under a canopy of leafy branches.

It was a delightful little chapel, but too small, Brother André's followers felt. "Don't worry," he confidently replied. "This is only the beginning."

Pilgrimages to the spot began, and the crowds continued to increase. The lay people associated with Brother André pressed for permission to enlarge the oratory further. Within a few years, an extension was built on the back of the chapel to shelter the faithful from sun and rain. In 1908, Brother André's associates enlarged the chapel further and installed a stove for heat.

By now, Brother André was able to receive visitors at the oratory, rather than the trolley shelter. In 1909 his community officially released him from all his duties at the school and named him "guardian of the oratory" on a full-time basis.

That year, some three thousand persons attended the blessing of the chapel's first bell, and more than twenty-nine thousand letters poured in from all over the world requesting Brother André's prayers. As his reputation as a healer spread, contributions to his ministry increased. Part of the funds were used to erect a small kiosk near the chapel. Brother André had an office and a small waiting room there for people who wished to see him. Soon after, the Blessed Sacrament was permanently reserved in the chapel, and the provincial appointed Father Adolphe Clément to provide full-time priestly ministry. Spurred by the growth of the oratory as a center of prayer and devotion to Saint Joseph, construction began on a residence for a full-time religious community there.

By now, hundreds of persons were visiting the oratory daily. Some days, during the summer months, as many as a thousand would come. Funding for new construction had ceased to be a problem and the congregation decided to build a large church on the spot. A contract was signed with an architectural firm and, in 1915, work began on the crypt of the new church. The crypt was completed and blessed two-and-a-half years later, replacing the original wooden chapel.

Pilgrims who visited the shrine frequently told of wonderful events that they had witnessed there. In 1916, four hundred thirty-five cures were recorded. Visitors returned home telling of having seen dying persons restored to health, or cripples casting aside crutches which had suddenly become useless to them. In some cases, the claims were backed up by the testimony of medical professionals.

Doctors cited unexplainable, sudden cures of several "hopeless" cases of advanced tuberculosis. Dr. L.O. Gauthier and Dr. W. Beaupré, both of Quebec, gave written statements in the case of a girl named Marie Antoinette Mercier whose right eye had been destroyed in an accident. After a visit to Saint Joseph's Oratory, the sight in the "destroyed" eye became normal. Dr. Beaupré declared that "the finger of God" was "manifest in this cure."

Some medical professionals, however, ridiculed Brother André as a charlatan or a fool. Dr. Joseph Charette, a devout Catholic, was revolted by such seemingly superstitious practices as rubbing patients with medals or Saint Joseph's oil. But when his wife developed a serious nosebleed, neither Dr. Charette nor several other doctors could stop the flow of blood.

"Bring Brother André," Mrs. Charette demanded.

Feeling foolish, the embarrassed doctor set off for the shrine to seek help from the man he had ridiculed. Brother André welcomed him and said, "Doctor, return home; your wife's nosebleed has stopped." It had.

George Ham, a Protestant visitor who worked as public relations officer of the Canadian Pacific Railway, claimed to have seen miracles take place at the shrine. Ham, an educated and sophisticated man of the world, even claimed that some oil from the shrine, taken to London by a friend, had worked a miraculous cure there.

Brother André remained as simple and unpretentious as ever. He never took credit for any of the cures. "I am nothing," he would say. "I have done nothing. It is the good Saint Joseph who does it all."

By the time he was in his eighties, Brother André, wrinkled with age and weighing no more than one hundred ten pounds, was receiving about eight thousand pilgrims a week. He rose each morning in time for meditation with his community at five-thirty. After assisting at Mass, he usually spent the rest of the morning receiving visitors. His office, in a pavilion near the shrine, measured about eleven feet by six feet. It was partitioned off from the candy shop and a tearoom used by the visitors. The floor and walls were of wood. A yellow counter separated the pilgrims from Brother André, who sat on a tall chair, dressed in a threadbare cassock.

One at a time, the pilgrims entered his office and he would greet them: "What is it you want?"

As the visitor answered, Brother André, who was growing deaf, would bring his ear close to the speaker's mouth, straining to hear each word and listening sympathetically to the prayer request. When the visitor finished speaking, Brother André would usually reply, "I will pray for you. Have you the Saint Joseph's medal? Rub yourself with oil and the medal of Saint Joseph. Make a novena to Saint Joseph and pray to him much."

And so it would go, until the morning was gone. Shortly before noon he would again pray with his community, and then have a light meal. In the afternoon he would return to his office to receive more visitors, but his ministry to the sick didn't end there. In the evening, working from a list prepared by his superior, he would set out to visit those whose infirmities made it difficult or impossible to come to see him.

Christ was the center of Brother André's life and André maintained his relationship with Jesus by intense devotion to Mary and Joseph. If he was not otherwise occupied or asleep, he usually prayed the rosary. Every day he found time to make the way of the cross; and as time went by, others joined him. He frequently visited the Blessed Sacrament and spent many hours in prayer before the tabernacle.

Construction of the great basilica which now stands on Mount Royal began in 1924, but the great depression of the 1930s halted the project for many years. In 1936, twelve years after the project had started, and twenty years after the crypt had replaced the wooden chapel, the basilica still didn't even have a roof. Brother André, now ninety-one, suggested that a statue of Saint Joseph be placed in the unfinished building. With his characteristic simple faith in the intercession of his patron, Brother André explained, "If Saint Joseph wants to put a roof over his head, he will take care of it."

The exterior of the basilica was completed by the end of the following year, but Brother André did not live that long. On December 27, 1936, he suffered an attack of indigestion so severe that he became bedridden. His suffering grew worse and he was hospitalized on New Year's Eve. The next evening, his right arm became paralyzed. In agony, he murmured, "What suffering! My God, my God!"

Father Thomas Barrosse, as superior general of the Congregation of Holy Cross, wrote a short biography of Brother André describing how, in his last few hours of consciousness, Brother André suddenly began speaking of his work and the oratory — two subjects which he ordinarily was too modest to mention.

"I was the right one for that," Brother André said. "I had to be everything: lawyer, doctor, priest. . . . But the good Lord was helping. See how powerful the good Lord is! How beautiful! . . . Yes, how beautiful because the soul, just a reflection of his beauty, is so beautiful!" His last words, before slipping into a coma, were, "This is the seed. . . ."

At 12:50 A.M. on Wednesday, January 6, the feast of the Epiphany, while thousands prayed for him, the Miracle Man of Montreal stopped breathing.

For a week, despite the severe Canadian winter, an estimated one million people came to the oratory to pay their respects. Some had to stand in line for at least four hours before they reached his body. Special trains brought mourners from distant cities and towns, and newspapers throughout Canada, the United States, and elsewhere focused the world's attention on these events. Many cures were reported among the crowds who came. Thousands received the sacrament of penance, keeping priests busy in ten confessionals.

Brother André's funeral was huge. The funeral sermon was preached by the cardinal-archbishop of Quebec City, the primate of Canada. Bishops were there, along with the premier of the province and the mayor of Montreal.

Since the death of the Miracle Man, the interior of the basilica has been completed. The basilica is a tangible reminder of the greatness and the healing power of Christ that can flow through the humblest and weakest of his children.

On May 23, 1982, Pope John Paul II beatified Brother André in Rome, holding him up to the Church as someone who had lived a heroic life in Christ — a life worthy of being revered and imitated by other Christians.

8

The Healer from America's Heartland

Father Solanus Casey was as practical and as down-to-earth as the rich Wisconsin soil which he helped his father till. He was a farmer, logger, prison guard, trolleycar motorman, country fiddler, and priest.

Thousands also knew this Capuchin priest as a healer, although Father Solanus didn't really consider himself one. He felt he had little to do with the hundreds of healings attributed to him. He insisted that he had simply listened to people's prayer requests and offered Masses for them. When people tearfully praised him for making them well, he declared that he had done nothing. "Jesus made you well through the power of the Mass," he would tell them.

He wore a somewhat unruly beard, and his blue eyes twinkled with a rare sense of humor and practical wisdom. He was a humble man, devoted to the sick and the poor. He would spend hours consoling and comforting visitors. He was never too busy to see them. Usually he signed his letters, "Solanus, sinner — Homo Simplex."

The "simple man" was born on November 25, 1870, in a two-room log cabin on a farm near the Mississippi River outside Prescott, Wisconsin. His parents, devout Irish Catholic immigrants, took him to St. Patrick's Church in nearby Hudson where he was baptized Bernard Francis Casey. His father, James Casey, had previously lived in Massachusetts where he made shoes for the Union Army during the Civil War; after the war, he and his bride, Ellen Elizabeth Murphy, moved to Wisconsin to try farming.

Bernard, or "Barney," as his family called him, was the sixth of sixteen children. When he was a child he suffered a serious case of diphtheria — a disease which in those days was often fatal. Barney survived, but for years afterward he suffered a throat ailment that weakened his vocal cords.

Jim and Ellen Casey worked hard to take care of their large family. Sometimes the harvests were good and sometimes they failed. In any event, the couple provided a happy home that was secure in love if not in material wealth. In later years, Barney and his brothers and sisters would always remember those days on the farm with fondness and nostalgia; the parents, on the other hand, recalled more vividly the struggle to survive.

Like Brother André, Barney received much of his religious training from his mother. She taught him devotion to the Blessed Virgin Mary, and Barney (after working long hours helping his father in the fields) would kneel at night to say the rosary. Over the years, his devotion to Mary would bloom until it was one of his strongest spiritual traits.

Once, in his youth, he dreamed that he was hanging over a fire but was saved from burning when he grabbed a large rosary suspended above his head. The rosary held and he never let go. After that dream, he vowed he would say the rosary daily.

Barney grew up tall, lanky, and fond of all kinds of sports except boxing. He liked music too. Once, a visitor inadvertently left a violin at the Casey home and didn't come back for it. Eventually, Barney picked up the instrument and began teaching himself to play jigs and reels that he learned from his Irish parents.

While he was still in the district school, Barney began earning money to help meet his family's expenses. One summer, he went to Stillwater, Minnesota, where he got a job as a lumberjack on the St. Croix River steering logs into the lumber mills there. It was twenty miles from his home, so he spent nights with his mother's brother, Father Maurice Murphy, pastor of the local Catholic church. The money that Barney earned that summer helped pay his family's debts after the wheat harvest failed.

Because of the time he had spent helping his family on the farm, he was seventeen before he finished eighth grade in 1887. Instead of continuing his education, he went to work, first at a brick kiln and then at the state penitentiary in Stillwater where he worked as a guard.

His liking for people and his sensitivity to the needs of the prisoners made him popular with the inmates. Among the prisoners with whom he developed a friendship were Jim and Cole Younger, former members of Jesse James's gang.

He left his prison job to work as a motorman for Stillwater's new trolley system. While living in Stillwater, he dated and fell in love with Rebecca Tobin, a former classmate. He asked her to marry him, but her mother opposed the idea and sent her away to a boarding school. Barney never saw her again.

Barney continued to work as a trolley motorman, in Appleton, Wisconsin, and later in the booming port city of Superior. His family was still having financial troubles, but Barney and his brothers persuaded their father that there were opportunities to earn more money in Superior. Jim Casey took his sons' advice. With Barney's brothers, he acquired a forty-acre dairy farm close to Superior and built a house in the heart of town so that the younger children could attend parochial school.

Barney, as a young man, remained a faithful Catholic, accustomed to daily prayer. As his family's financial situation improved, he began to seriously consider the possibility that God was calling him to the priesthood. It was an idea that had persisted for years, but he had never done more than think about it. On one occasion, while he was driving his trolley, something happened that awoke in him a new awareness of evil and suffering in the world.

There was a crowd on the tracks ahead. He brought the streetcar to a halt and got out to investigate. At the center of the crowd, a woman lay bleeding from many stab wounds. A drunken sailor waving a bloody knife stood over her, cursing. Awful moments passed until two policemen arrived and disarmed the assailant at gunpoint.

The images of that violent act haunted Barney, who saw them as symbolic of all the hatred, all the sin, and all the suffering of the world. He believed that in some manner he must bring healing to the wounds of humanity. Two days after the stabbing incident, he visited the pastor of Sacred Heart Church, who agreed to sponsor him at St. Francis de Sales Seminary, a German institution in Milwaukee.

He arrived in Milwaukee in the winter of 1892. He studied hard, but his courses, particularly Latin and German, proved more difficult than he had thought they would be. At first he held his own, but when his grades began to fall, his superiors told him they didn't think he could meet the academic challenges still to come. They assured him that they thought he had a religious vocation, but they asked him to leave.

He was confused by this seeming contradiction. Not knowing what to do or where to go, he went home. But he grew restless and sought advice from Father Eustace Vollmer, a Franciscan priest, who suggested that Barney apply to the Franciscan Capuchin seminary in Detroit. Barney balked at the idea. Capuchins were committed to a rigorous monastic life and wore beards, which in those days looked bizarre to clean-cut young Midwesterners like Barney. Becoming a Capuchin didn't appeal to him, but he agreed to pray about it.

At Sacred Heart Church in Superior, he began a novena to Mary Immaculate and on December 8, 1896, wrote in his notebook, "Vow of chastity — and at once. Decision in vocation to Detroit. Deo gratias." Later he explained that he had become convinced during the novena that Mary was telling him, "Go to Detroit."

He left Superior on December 21. He sat up through two nights on trains that crept from St. Paul to Chicago while a severe Midwestern winter buried the tracks. On Christmas Eve, cold and weary, he knocked at the door of St. Bonaventure's Monastery in Detroit. The porter took him in and led him to a cell where he lay down and, wondering what he was doing there, fell asleep. He awoke to the strains of "Adeste Fideles" and went to the chapel to sing carols with the friars.

It was a glad and peaceful Christmas, but soon after, he began doubting that this was where he should be. The friars had given him a copy of the *Rule of St. Francis* which he was to study. The writings of the little saint of Assisi didn't alleviate Barney's gloom and he scribbled on the flyleaf, "January 13, 1897. Dark indeed." But his agony was to last only one more day. On January 14, when he entered the chapel to ask for the brown habit, his sorrow turned to joy. He was invested as a novice and was given the religious name, Frater Francis Solanus, O.F.M. Capuchin.

On July 21, 1898, he made his simple profession of vows and after that he was sent back to Milwaukee to resume his studies, this time at St. Francis of Assisi Capuchin Seminary.

Again, he had trouble keeping up academically. His

books were written in Latin and the seminary professors explained them in German. His grades were below average and some of the faculty wanted to hold him back. But Father Anthony Rottensteiner, a former provincial who had become head of the theological faculty at the seminary, tutored him privately and certified him to receive tonsure, the ceremony by which a lay person prepares for minor orders and becomes a cleric.

"We shall ordain Solanus," Father Rottensteiner predicted, "and as a priest he shall be to the people something like the Curé of Ars."

He was ordained a priest on July 24, 1904, at St. Francis Church in Milwaukee, but under conditions which were to place limits on his ministry. The faculty recognized him as a person of extraordinary spirituality and practical ability; but, for reasons that are not fully clear, the faculty voted that he was to remain forever a *sacerdos simplex*, able to celebrate the Mass but forbidden to hear confessions or to preach formal sermons on theology or doctrine. On the surface, at least, it would appear that the faculty felt Father Solanus's theological understanding was too weak for the pulpit or the confessional — and although the "simple priest" had achieved passing grades in Church dogma, his marks were slightly below average.

Whatever the reasons for imposing them, the limitations were seen by some of Father Solanus's fellow Capuchins as a blessing in disguise. "He had such utter disregard for time, and such boundless compassion, that he would have heard one confession to my ten," one of them said. "Moreover, his horror of mortal sin was such that I am sure some confessions would have caused him almost unbearable shock and sorrow."

Under the conditions imposed at his ordination, Father Solanus could and did give informal devotional homilies, but he could give absolution only to persons in danger of death. His inability to hear confessions or preach stayed with him all his life. He never held any position of responsibility in the order. His assignments were the kind usually given to brothers, not priests. He was given the role of sacristan and, like Brother André, porter. He was in charge of answering the door, supplying linens for the church, arranging the altar, and watching over the altar boys.

Even though he was not permitted to give doctrinal sermons, he conversed comfortably with brilliant theologians and scholars. "His conversation was that of one inspired by the Holy Spirit," said Dr. A.L. Gabriel, O. Praem., of the Institute of Medieval Studies at Notre Dame University. "I found him most inspiring. Each time I visited him, I left richer than before."

The limitations imposed on his ministry were "a humiliation and a cross," according to one of the Capuchins who knew him well. Yet Father Solanus accepted them with humility and without complaint. In doing so, he reached a sanctity which some said he could not have attained in any other way.

The fact that he was not allowed to preach or hear confessions deepened his appreciation of his faculty for celebrating the Eucharist — an undisputed sign of his priesthood. From the earliest days of his priesthood, his celebration of the Mass was closely linked to his ability to inspire others. When Father Solanus celebrated his first Mass, his older brother Maurice, who had also been a seminary dropout, was so moved that he decided to return to the seminary.

Despite his lowly assignments, Father Solanus was admired and respected. When he was assigned to Sacred Heart Friary in Yonkers, New York, in 1904, visitors were surprised to find a priest instead of a brother "on the door." But they soon discovered him to be a compassionate listener who cared about people. Increasing numbers came to the friary just to talk to him. Instead of hearing confessions and giving absolution, he developed a hallway ministry in which he listened to problems and offered prayers. Sometimes he would spend long periods counseling people over the telephone. On at least one occasion, a member of his community found him late at night trying to cheer someone by playing his fiddle into the telephone.

In 1921, at Our Lady of Angels Friary in Harlem, Father Solanus took on what appeared to be yet another minor task. His superior appointed him to promote the Seraphic Mass Association, the enrollment of donors in Capuchin Mass intentions. Part of the funds given by the donors supported the Capuchin missions, and because Father Solanus strongly supported missionary work, he put his whole heart into the project.

It was at that point that something unusual began to happen. Large numbers of the people whom Father Solanus was enrolling in the association began telling of healings, conversions, and other marvelous answers to their Mass intentions. By November 8, 1923, these reports had reached the Capuchin provincial and he ordered Father Solanus to begin keeping records of the prayer requests of the enrollees. The *sacerdos simplex* recorded not only the requests but encouraged the enrollees to let him know about ways in which their Mass intentions had been answered. His records were entered in a twelve-by-ten-inch ledger titled "Notes About Special Cases," and over the next three decades he filled seven such ledgers with more than six thousand notations. To about seven hundred of these, he later added footnotes reporting cures, conversions, and other answers to prayer requests.

His notations typically began with thanks to God: "Deo gratias. Marg Quinn enrolled neighbor Mr._____ against drink and consequent anger October 26 — and also her sister E. Remy of Philadelphia against severe inflammatory rheumatism — reports wonderful improvement in former and letter this morning from sister says 'Thanks to God & good prayer society, I'm feeling fine.'"

Some of the entries describe more dramatic events. One of these involved a woman who had lost her memory for eight years as a result of a concussion. Two days after Solanus enrolled her in the Mass League, her husband reported that her memory had been restored.

Most of the prayer requests came to Father Solanus by mail, but there were cures too among those who came to the monastery to see him. One of his ledger entries reports the case of a forty-six-year-old man who had been carried into the monastery with a broken back he had suffered a few weeks earlier in an accident. "Walking out of the monastery without assistance" is the notation that follows the entry.

Other entries record the recovery of persons confined to mental institutions, the restoration of peace between former enemies, and the return of loved ones to the sacraments. "Papa went to confession and Communion for the first time in 39 years," wrote a girl whom Father Solanus had enrolled.

Whenever people tried to thank him, he would remind them of the power of the Mass and tell them to give thanks to God. But the people tended, nevertheless, to see the "simple priest" as instrumental in obtaining answers to their prayers.

"He spoke so quietly that they may not have understood what he was talking about," suggests Father Bernard Burke, a former superior of Father Solanus. "The point is, he listened to them, and that's what they came for."

His superiors, who wanted to observe Father Solanus at work, transferred him in 1924 to St. Bonaventure Monastery in Detroit, where he had originally been invested as a novice. He remained at St. Bonaventure's for twenty-one years, continuing his priestly career of doorkeeper and enroller of Seraphic Mass Association donors. He was assigned to assist one of the brothers who served both as porter and tailor, but his light was shining more brightly than ever and could not be hidden by these humble assignments.

His ministry of prayer and counseling expanded. He had an office now in which he could receive visitors from seven in the morning until ten at night. He received people seven days a week, treating each person as the most important person in the world.

Many simply wanted his blessing. Others came to discuss spiritual matters. Young people sought his guidance in choosing a vocation. He spent much time with sick children, listening so intently to their needs and problems that he often was late for chapel devotions.

During the years at St. Bonaventure's, he began to manifest what have been referred to as his "predictions." Sometimes, speaking with great certainty, he would accurately tell people what to expect in answer to their prayers. Usually these were simple statements, such as "Your child will get well." But sometimes they specifically predicted cures. In one case a person asking prayers for a sick person was told, "There will be a change at nine o'clock."

Perhaps the most startling prediction involved a man named John Regan who worked in the composing room of *The Detroit News*. Regan's face and eyes had been badly burned when molten typecasting lead had been accidentally splashed upon his face. A doctor who had examined him at Harper Hospital declared that Regan was "permanently blinded." Regan's wife went to Father Solanus, who listened tenderly to her and finally told her, "Don't worry. John will see. He has not lost his sight. I will have Mass offered for him in the morning."

When the bandages were removed from Regan's eyes, the same doctor who had declared him blind was astounded to discover that Regan's vision was normal. "If ever I saw a miracle, this is one," the doctor declared.

Father Solanus's predictions weren't always

cheerful. "Be resigned and place your wife in the arms of God," he advised a man whose wife had just undergone a minor operation. The woman later died.

During the great depression of the 1930s, Father Solanus's community operated a soup kitchen where he helped in both ordinary and extraordinary ways. Through his counseling ministry, he had acquired many friends on whom he could call to give someone a ride, to pick up a load of donated food, or do any other chores involved. Father Solanus would talk to the men, join them in line for food, and eat with them. He also knew how to trust God when supplies were running low. On one occasion, when he was told that there was no more bread, he turned in the direction of the kitchen, made the sign of the cross, and said, "Have confidence." Moments later, a a deliveryman pushed a big basket of bread into the kitchen and said, "I've got a lot more in the truck."

As Father Solanus got older, his long hours of counseling began to tire him beyond his endurance. In 1945, shortly before his seventy-fifth birthday, he was transferred to St. Michael's Friary in Brooklyn, New York, and the following year to St. Felix Friary, the order's novitiate house in Huntington, Indiana, where he was ordered to retire.

He tried to. He loved the country. He worked in the garden, where the warmth of the sun and the rich earth made him remember the simple pleasures of his Wisconsin boyhood. He was known as "Father Beekeeper." But it wasn't long before petitioners from all over the Midwest began descending on the friary, sometimes by the busload.

His superiors tried to protect him from the strain of seeing them. He felt torn between obedience to his superiors and his ministry. "Why don't they let me see the people?" he asked.

He became seriously ill in 1956 and was sent back to St. Bonaventure's. During this last illness, he spoke often of the world's need for conversion, declaring, "I cannot die before all people are united to know and love God." On July 30, 1957, after days of immobility, he declared, "Tomorrow will be a wonderful day." It was the last of his predictions. Shortly before his death, he opened his eyes and said clearly, "I give my soul to Jesus Christ." Father Solanus died July 31, 1957, in St. John's Hospital, Detroit, at the age of eighty-seven.

An estimated twenty thousand people passed by his coffin before he was laid to rest on August 3. Soon after his death, the Father Solanus Guild was organized in his memory to carry on his work for the poor and the ill and to work for his cause of beatification. The guild has more than five thousand members in the United States, Canada, Europe, and Australia.

On June 19, 1982, Pope John Paul II permitted the introduction of Father Solanus's cause. In October of 1984, testimony from fifty-three priests, religious, and lay persons who knew Father Solanus Casey was presented in Rome to the Sacred Congregation for the Causes of Saints. At this writing, the congregation is in the process of reviewing and evaluating evidence that this simple son of the American soil is worthy of veneration as a Christian hero.

9

The Healing Ministry
of Padre Pio

The best-known Catholic healer of the twentieth century was a man named Francesco Forgione, who was born in the late 1800s in the town of Pietrelcina in south-central Italy. The world knows him better as Padre Pio.

Like Saint Paul, he was known as a miracle worker; like Anthony of the Desert, he engaged in an ongoing battle against satanic forces; like Saint Catherine and Saint Francis, he embraced suffering and was marked with the wounds of Jesus. His similarity to Saint Francis was so pronounced that many persons called him "a second Saint Francis."

But unlike Francis, Padre Pio is a man of our own century, a person whose reputation as a healer isn't clouded by the mists of time. The healings attributed to him weren't reported by medieval biographers but by modern journalists and authors, including some who could hardly be considered propagandists for the Church. Articles about his ministry have appeared in *Time*, *Newsweek*, and the magazine section of the *New York Times*. Hundreds of other articles and a number of books about him have been published in his native Italy and elsewhere. Many people still living knew him and have given detailed accounts of how they were healed through his prayers.

Padre Pio, like Father Solanus and Brother André, became famous as a healer in an age when most people sought healing from doctors instead of through prayer. Because his international reputation as a healer contradicted the prevailing scientific view of sickness and healing, Padre Pio's healings were closely scrutinized. Throughout the world, people wanted to know whether this unusual friar was a charlatan or a man endowed by God with the ability to work miracles.

His reputation as a healer wasn't the only thing that set Padre Pio apart from others. He exercised the charismatic gift of prophecy and may have also had the gift of speaking in tongues, a gift commonly exercised among charismatics and Pentecostals but rarely among Catholics during the time when he lived.

He had an uncanny ability to know the thoughts of others. When he heard confessions, for example, he frequently astounded total strangers by reminding them of long-forgotten sins which they had neglected to confess. This "gift of knowledge," like the gifts of healing, prophecy, speaking in tongues, and the ability to work miracles, is among the gifts of the Holy Spirit described by Saint Paul in his First Letter to the Corinthians (12:8-10).

Yet Padre Pio, according to many who knew him, manifested other extraordinary phenomena which are not among the gifts cited by Paul. One was the gift of bilocation — the ability to physically appear in two places at the same time. Another was his "odor of sanctity," a perfumelike scent, similar to the smell of roses or violets, which was frequently noticed by persons in his presence, although Padre Pio wore no perfume or cologne. Some witnesses claim to have received healings or visions which they attribute to Padre Pio because even though he was not physically present, they could smell this distinctive odor.

For much of his life, Padre Pio was the center of controversy so intense that it occasionally erupted in violence. At least two popes, Pius XII and Paul VI, indicated privately that they considered him a saint, but some high Church officials considered him mentally unbalanced if not a fraud. Others viewed him as a holy man but one whose spiritual gifts had been exaggerated and embellished by superstitious followers.

Francesco Forgione was born just before the beginning of the twentieth century, in a part of Italy where superstition and faith were still closely intertwined. His mother, Maria Giuseppa Forgione (affectionately known as Beppa), was a devout and pious Catholic, yet each time she bore a child she would take the baby to a man named Faiella, the neighborhood fortune-teller, who would cast the child's horoscope.

Francesco was born on May 25, 1887, the fourth

child of Beppa and her husband, Grazio, a puritanical but jovial farmer known for his piety and his ability as a storyteller. Neither Beppa nor Grazio could read or write, but they were hardworking, practical people with good minds and devout hearts.

According to Beppa, Francesco cried incessantly when he was a baby. The reasons for his crying spells aren't known, but Padre Pio himself has said he can remember being tormented by "monsters" when his mother would turn down the lamp. He insisted that "it was the devil who was tormenting me." Such torments were to continue throughout most of his life.

But that darker side of his spirituality didn't dominate his life. As a child, he enjoyed school, tended his family's sheep, and enjoyed pretending that he was a priest celebrating Mass. Like other boys, he could be mischievous, but he was better known for his unusual obedience and piety. In later years, he said he had always wanted to be a priest. Like that of Catherine of Siena, his childhood included some unusual spiritual experiences, although they did not seem particularly unusual to him. Sometimes these involved conversations with his guardian angel and sometimes with Jesus or the Virgin Mary.

He told his parents when he was ten that he wanted to be a "monk" like the bearded Capuchin friar who regularly visited Pietrelcina soliciting food for the friary in nearby Morcone.

When Grazio Forgione saw that his son was serious, he began sending the boy to private schools to prepare him for the studies he would have to undertake to become a priest. Forgione also made sure that there would be enough money to pay for his son's studies. He traveled to America in 1897 and worked on a farm in Pennsylvania, sending money home regularly for Francesco's education.

Just before he entered the Capuchin order in 1903, Francesco had a series of visions which he understood as a sign that his priesthood would be a long struggle against the devil, but with Jesus at his side. He was sixteen when he entered the friary and took, as his new religious name, "Pio," Italian for Pius, after Saint Pius V, a sixteenth-century pope.

The Capuchin order was the most conservative of the Franciscan orders of Religious men. The life of its friars was filled not only with prayer but with practices that, by today's standards, seem harsh and medieval. Three times a week, the friars lashed themselves with chains to strengthen their spirits against laziness and sexual passion. Padre Tommaso, the novice-master, is said to have sometimes ordered the novices, including Pio, to whip themselves until their blood ran onto the floor.

Pio, a model novice, lived in utter obedience to his superiors and endured such rigorous exercises without complaint. He was extremely submissive and prayerful, yet almost always cheerful. In spite of the harsh discipline, he never lost his boyhood love of jokes and pranks.

Like Catherine of Siena and Brother André, he was unable to eat normally. From the beginning of his novitiate he was plagued by mysterious but intense vomiting, accompanied by constipation, coughing, headaches, and fevers. He made his permanent vows in 1906; but because of his health, he was given permission to live at home in Pietrelcina — where his health improved. Yet whenever he returned to the friary, his symptoms reappeared. He was examined by several doctors, one of whom thought he was suffering from tuberculosis, but the others found no trace of the disease.

In spite of his chronic poor health, which forced him to live almost without eating, he returned to the friary and was ordained to the diaconate in early 1909. Soon after, he collapsed and was again sent home. As before, he improved, but when he returned to his community, he suffered more vomiting and violent cramps. At home once more, he suspected that God was for some reason thwarting his desire to live in community.

Pio saw it as punishment for some unknown and unconfessed sin; but his confessor, Padre Benedetto Nardella, wrote to him, "Your sufferings are not punishment, but rather ways of earning merit that the Lord is giving you, and the shadows that weigh on your soul are generated by the devil, who wants to harm you." He cautioned the young deacon that "the closer God draws to a soul, the more the enemy troubles him."

On August 10, 1910, while he was still living at home, Pio was ordained to the priesthood by Archbishop Paolo Schinosi in the Cathedral of Benevento. The day of his ordination was the happiest he had ever known.

During the early days of his priesthood, while Pio was living in Pietrelcina, his writings revealed what was to become a distinguishing character of his ministry — a desire to share fully in the suffering of Christ. He described himself as "a holy priest, a perfect victim." In a letter to his friend and confidant, Padre Agostine Daniele, Pio wrote: "[The Lord] chose certain souls, and among them, despite my unworthiness, He also chose me, to assist in the great work of the salvation of mankind. The more these souls suffer without any consolation, to that extent are the pains of our good Jesus made the lighter. This is why I want to suffer increasingly and without comfort. And this is all my joy. It is only too true that I need courage, but Jesus will deny me nothing."

During this same period Padre Pio went to Father Salvatore Maria Pannullo, his pastor in Pietrelcina, and showed him puncture wounds that had appeared in the palms of his hands. Pio told him that while he had been praying, Jesus and Mary had given him the wounds.

Two doctors examined the wounded hands. The first told Pio he had "tuberculosis of the skin." The second doctor disagreed but could not explain the cause of the wounds. Padre Pio was embarrassed by them and asked Father Pannullo to pray with him "to ask Jesus to take away this annoyance." Father Pannullo told Pio he must be willing to bear the wounds if that is what Jesus desired. Nevertheless, the two men prayed and, for a time, the wounds disappeared.

When World War I broke out, the Italian government began drafting even priests to serve in the army. Despite his bad health, Pio was inducted in November 1915. But his health grew worse and he was permitted to return home. Eventually, at the urging of Padre Benedetto, Pio returned to the friary of St. Anne, in

Foggia, where he remained constantly sick, nearly unable to eat, and subject to what he described as diabolical attacks, accompanied by loud crashing noises which alarmed other members of the community.

Pio was given permission in 1916 to move to the friary at Our Lady of Grace at San Giovanni Rotondo in the Gargano Mountains, where it was hoped the cooler mountain air would make him more comfortable. His stay there was interrupted briefly when the army called him to duty. But soon he was unable to eat and he was given another military leave of absence. On March 16, 1918, he was discharged permanently for what had been diagnosed as bronchial problems. He returned to San Giovanni Rotondo. It was from this remote community in the mountains of Italy that Padre Pio's fame as a confessor, healer, and miracle worker spread throughout the world.

Literally thousands of healings have been attributed to Padre Pio's prayers. Some of these seem miraculous and others do not. An eyewitness account given to me by Joan Markey of Norway, Maine, seems fairly typical. It occurred after she took her fifteen-month-old baby, Gerard, to San Giovanni Rotondo in 1959.

"We were living in Italy at the time, because my husband, Andrew, was stationed in Naples," she said.

Gerard had been born in Italy with a circulatory problem that left him weak. "He had a heart murmur and a slight hole in his heart," his mother said. Sometimes his hands would turn blue. Unlike other children, he didn't use his legs. He had not yet begun to crawl, let alone walk. The child's inability to use his legs seemed to be related to his circulatory disorders, but doctors in Naples were at a loss to do anything about it.

The Markeys decided to take him to specialists in Germany, but Mrs. Markey decided she would first take Gerard to San Giovanni Rotondo. The boy's doctors, who knew of Padre Pio's reported cures, agreed with her decision, and she went there the weekend after Thanksgiving, hoping that perhaps the saintly friar would pray for the success of the trip to Germany.

When she got to the monastery an American priest named Father Domenic answered the door. "I explained that we just wanted Padre Pio's blessing and prayers," she said. That evening, after Benediction, Father Domenic called Mrs. Markey aside and told her that Padre Pio would see the baby after Mass the next morning.

"The next day, Father Domenic took us into the little chapel where Padre Pio heard confessions," she said. "The door opened and Padre Pio came through it." To Mrs. Markey he looked like "an old, humble, hard-working Italian man" who had some difficulty walking.

She tells how she handed the baby to Father Domenic and how the baby began crying. So he gave the baby back to her and led her over to Padre Pio, who smiled, looked down at the baby, and asked in Italian, "The baby can't walk?" Since she spoke some Italian, she understood what he was saying and told him "yes," that was the baby's problem.

Mrs. Markey went on to tell me: "He put his hand on the baby's head. He said, 'The baby will walk soon.' He turned and started to walk away. Then he came back and put his hand out — for me to kiss it, I guess." Mrs. Markey knelt and kissed the extended left hand while Padre Pio, who was wearing gloves, blessed her with the other.

Filled with gratitude and faith, Mrs. Markey abandoned her plans to take Gerard to the specialists in Germany. Between Christmas Day and New Year's, she and her husband were entertaining guests in their apartment in Naples when one of the visitors stepped from the living room into the hall and shouted, "Oh, my God!"

Unobserved, the usually immobile Gerard had somehow moved from the living room and was standing in the hall. While the amazed grown-ups watched, the child walked the length of the hall.

Although the circulatory problem was never completely cured, Gerard is now in his twenties and leading a normal life.

What happened to Gerard is similar to, although less dramatic than, what had happened to a cripple named Francesco Santarello during the early years of Padre Pio's ministry. Santarello, a pathetic, clubfooted man, was a familiar sight in San Giovanni Rotondo, where he was regarded as the village idiot and was taunted and tormented by cruel youngsters.

One day, while Santarello was begging near the door to the cloister, Padre Pio passed by on his way to church.

"Padre Pio, give me a blessing!" the poor man cried out.

"Throw away your crutches," Pio replied without a moment's hesitation. In front of a crowd of people, Santarello tossed the crutches away and never used them again, although his feet remained deformed.

In both the Markey and the Santarello healings, Padre Pio's prayers were credited with overcoming a handicap without fully restoring the patient's health. There were many other instances in which complete cures were attributed to Padre Pio. Many of these healings are described in detail in C. Bernard Ruffin's excellent *Padre Pio: The True Story*, published by Our Sunday Visitor.

One of the more remarkable cases is the cure of Dr. Francesco Ricciardi, a man who disavowed any belief in God and who supported those who publicly mocked Padre Pio. In the fall of 1928, Dr. Ricciardi was diagnosed by five doctors who agreed that he was hopelessly ill with incurable stomach cancer. By December, he was near death.

One of his best friends, a priest, tried to visit the dying man but was turned away. "I intend to die as I have lived," Ricciardi insisted. Yet he allowed Padre Pio to see him in private. It is not known what Padre Pio said or did, but when the family was readmitted, the doctor had confessed his sins, received Holy Communion, and was now weeping and embracing Padre Pio.

"Father, bless me one more time," they heard him say. Believing that there was no chance he would recover, the dying man continued, "There is no more hope for me, and in a little while I will be dead, and so I want to leave the world with your pardon and another blessing from you."

But Padre Pio replied, "Your soul is healed, and

soon your body will be healed as well! You will go to the friary and repay the visit that I have made this evening." Within three days, all signs of the cancer were gone. The physician lived another four years — as a practicing Catholic.

One of the best-known cures cited in Ruffin's biography is known as "the miracle of Ribera." Ribera is a town in Sicily where a little girl named Gemma DiGiorgio was born in 1939 with a strange congenital eye defect. She claims that as a child she was totally blind. "I had no pupils in my eyes. I had no sight at all," she declared when she was interviewed by another American writer, Father John A. Schug, in 1971. She told Father Schug that a famous oculist in Palermo had once told her mother that, without pupils, she would never be able to see.

In 1946, Gemma's grandmother took her to San Giovanni Rotondo where Padre Pio heard the child's first confession, administered First Communion, and made the sign of the cross on her eyes.

Father Schug declared that when he saw her in 1971, her eyes still had no pupils. "She looks like a blind person," he wrote, "But there is no doubt that she can see. I saw her reach for a phone book, check a number, and dial the number without groping. . . ."

It is not certain whether Gemma's vision had been nonexistent or simply defective before she visited Padre Pio; but after the visit, she could see normally.

One of the best-documented cures attributed to Padre Pio occurred in 1949 after Giovanni Savino, a construction worker, lost the sight of both eyes when a charge of dynamite accidentally exploded in his face.

Savino, a devout Franciscan tertiary, attended Padre Pio's Mass each morning. On the morning of February 12, 1949, Padre Pio blessed Savino as usual, but as he placed his hands on Savino's head, he said, "Courage! I'll pray to the Lord that it may not cause your death." Savino was alarmed but could not persuade Padre Pio to disclose what danger might lie ahead.

Three days later, the accident occurred. His left eye was badly damaged and his right eye was completely destroyed, leaving only a vacant socket.

He was hospitalized for three weeks as doctors tried to save the sight in his left eye. On the morning of February 25, as he lay in bed with his entire head and face bandaged, he felt something like a light slap on the right side of his face and asked, "Who touched me?" No one answered, but he said he smelled the distinctive aroma associated with Padre Pio.

When the bandages were removed, the doctors realized they had failed to save the vision in Savino's left eye. But they were baffled by the fact that Savino's right eye socket — the one which had been left empty by the explosion — was occupied by what seemed to be a normal eye. Savino never regained sight in his left eye but had normal vision in the right eye for the rest of his life.

Despite the cures, miraculous and otherwise, that were attributed to Padre Pio, the prayerful friar often declined to pray for cures and instead counseled ailing people to seek ordinary medical treatment. He respected the medical profession, although he would occasionally offer his own advice as to how doctors should treat a patient.

On one occasion, a woman named Mary Campanile, who belonged to a prayer group directed by Padre Pio, informed him that her mother was ill with double pneumonia and that doctors had applied leeches to draw her blood — a common medical practice in Italy at the time.

"She must not be bled," shouted Padre Pio. Although he had not seen or examined the sick woman, he insisted she was suffering from malaria, not pneumonia. Mary Campanile directed the doctors to remove the leeches, and her mother recovered.

Although millions of people throughout the world revered Padre Pio as a holy man of prayer, more often than not he was the center of controversy. He had enemies both within and outside the Church who called him a charlatan. Some of his detractors accused Padre Pio and other members of his community of deliberately faking miracles in order to call attention to Padre Pio and to attract donations of money from gullible believers. Some of his detractors claimed that Padre Pio was possessed by the devil.

As Padre Pio's fame spread, unruly crowds pushed and shoved to gain entrance to the Masses he celebrated at San Giovanni Rotondo.

In 1926, the Vatican's Holy Office, now known as the Congregation for the Doctrine of the Faith, felt obliged to investigate the many complaints it was receiving about Padre Pio and his controversial ministry. The Holy Office decreed that year that it "did not attest to the supernaturalness of the events" attributed to

Padre Pio and exhorted the faithful to "refrain from visiting him."

Padre Pio was directed to vary the hour of his daily Masses to discourage visitors, and he was forbidden to bless crowds from his window. He was told that he must not show his stigmata to visitors or, for that matter, even speak about the wounds. More restrictions were added in 1931 when the Holy Office ordered Pio stripped of all his priestly ministry except the faculty of celebrating the Mass. The restrictions remained in effect until 1933 when the Holy Office, after further investigation, revoked its decrees.

Although his healing gifts were responsible for much of the attention he received, many persons who met him were more impressed by his gifts as a confessor and by the intensity with which he celebrated the Eucharist.

During the years that he was permitted to see visitors, he welcomed everyone: Catholics, Protestants, members of non-Christian religions, and atheists.

His reputation as a healer wasn't limited to the miraculous. Toward the end of his life he worked tirelessly to establish a hospital called the Casa Sollievo della Sofferenza (Italian for "house for the alleviation of suffering").

From the start, Padre Pio rejected the idea of calling it a hospital — a name that he felt suggested suffering and death. His idea was to create ideal conditions for the care of the sick by providing both medical and spiritual healing.

Through donations and a $325,000 grant from the

United Nations Relief and Rehabilitation Administration, the five-story hospital opened in 1956. A *New York Times* reporter described it as "one of the most beautiful as well as one of the most modern and fully equipped hospitals in the world."

A striking fact about the life of Padre Pio was his desire to embrace suffering in his own life while alleviating the suffering of others. He wasn't a masochist — he didn't suffer for the sake of suffering but embraced it because he recognized suffering as an essential part of the life of Christ. Padre Pio reasoned that since it was only through suffering on the cross that Jesus was able to bring salvation to humanity, the priest should consider it a privilege, granted by Jesus, to share that mission.

Although Padre Pio sought to relieve the suffering of many, he apparently believed that it was not Christ's desire to heal everyone. He seemed to have an inner knowledge of whether it was God's desire to heal an individual or to strengthen that individual spiritually through the acceptance of suffering.

Padre Allesio Parente, a friar who assisted Padre Pio toward the end of his ministry, is quoted by Bernard Ruffin as saying: "I knew from experience that when Padre Pio said to the sick person, 'I'll pray for you' or 'Let's pray to God,'... [that individual] seemed always to be healed. On the other hand, if he said, 'Let's resign ourselves to the will of God,' or said nothing at all, the grace of healing was not to be."

Unlike charismatics in the healing ministry today, Padre Pio seldom laid hands on those for whom he prayed. In fact, most of the healings attributed to him took place away from his physical presence.

Many healings are attributed to Padre Pio's intercession because the person who was cured "saw" Pio or smelled his distinctive aroma, even though Pio was physically many miles away. When people thanked him for his intercession, he would often smile and say, "Don't thank me, thank God."

Padre Pio died on September 23, 1968. His body lies in a crypt beneath the main church of Our Lady of Grace at San Giovanni Rotondo. Nearly a million people a year still visit his tomb.

The cures attributed to him have never stopped. In fact, there have been as many since his death as there were during his many years at San Giovanni Rotondo. Every year, the friars there continue to receive letters which, time and again, tell the same story. Somewhere in the world someone was praying and received a visit from Padre Pio. Perhaps they saw him, or perhaps they simply smelled his unique odor of sanctity. But they insist that Padre Pio was there. He came to them and made them whole.

CONCLUSION
Healing as a Catholic Tradition

In the last few centuries, scientific discoveries have expanded human knowledge in all directions. Some of the greatest discoveries have been in the area of health and medicine. With greatly expanded scientific knowledge of our bodies and how they work, the people of the twentieth century possess an unprecedented ability to control disease and to promote health through medical practice based on science.

The greatest medical and scientific breakthroughs have been made within the last two or three generations. Many people now living can remember when influenza, diphtheria, smallpox, pneumonia, and polio claimed the lives of millions every year. This is no longer so. Through scientific research and modern medical practice, many diseases formerly considered incurable have virtually disappeared — at least in those nations whose people have access to modern medical practice. Many other diseases which used to be killers are still with us but are now easily cured with new drugs.

The western world has become a place of more or less continuous scientific discovery and medical breakthrough. It is not surprising that in such a world people are more likely to seek healing through doctors than through prayer.

It would be foolish to simply reject the curative powers that science and medicine provide. Wonder drugs, new understanding of the ways our bodies work, and new techniques for curing disease are all gifts from God. It was God who provided the substances from which the drugs were made and it was he who gave mankind the capacity to think, to observe the natural world, and to gradually unlock its secrets. The Old Testament wisely counsels believers to seek help first from God, but to recognize that one of the ways he heals is through those who practice medicine:

> My son, when you are sick, do not be negligent,
>> but pray to the Lord, and he will heal you. . . .
> And give the physician his place, for the Lord created him;
>> let him not leave you, for there is need of him.
>> — Sirach 38:9, 12

Medicine is indeed a gift from God, but in the last few centuries, there has been a tendency to adore the gift rather than the giver. Most people seek healing *only* through medicine. Many persons today regard scientific research as the one true path to truth and the medical profession as the exclusive source of healing. In essence, science and medicine have become twentieth-century idols.

And yet, in the midst of scientific achievement, we must recognize that modern medicine has its limits. It cannot yet cure every disease, as cancer and AIDS (Acquired Immune Deficiency Syndrome) patients are painfully aware. Meanwhile, during the past hundred years, Christians have been seeing a reawakening of the power through which the Church heals. Not since the second or third century have so many Catholics and Protestants embraced the idea that the healing ministry is an integral part of the Christian faith.

In churches, homes, auditoriums, football stadiums, parish halls, and television studios, clergy and Christian lay persons pray publicly and privately, asking Jesus, through the power of the Holy Spirit, to make the blind see and the lame walk. Catholic, Protestant, and secular publishers during the last two decades have published hundreds of books on the gift of healing and its place in the Church.

This renewal of the healing ministry has been growing rapidly among various Christian groups for the past century or so. Among Catholics of the early twentieth century, the power of healing was evident not only in the ministries of healers like Padre Pio, Father Solanus, and Brother André but also in the vast numbers of pilgrims who sought and found healing of body, mind, and spirit at the Marian shrine at Lourdes. During the same period, Pentecostals and related Protestant groups were experiencing what has been described as a renewal of the various gifts of the Holy Spirit, including the gift of healing.

For many years, Catholics and most mainline Protestants looked with distrust on Protestant healing services, which often seemed to be dominated by flamboyant ministers and showy theatrics. Some of these ministers showed little regard for the dignity or spiritual value of suffering, implying that suffering was something that need be endured only by those who lack sufficient faith in God's healing power. Most Catholics had little use for that brand of "faith healing."

But in the late 1960s and early 1970s, thousands of Catholics began to take the gift of healing more seriously. Catholic prayer groups began praying for a new "baptism in the Holy Spirit" and their members — like the Pentecostals — were soon claiming that God was working signs and wonders in their midst. Prayer for healing became a regular part of many Catholic charismatic prayer meetings. Reports of physical and spiritual healings were frequently reported, and individual members of Catholic prayer groups began to acquire reputations as healers.

By the 1980s, the healing ministries of Catholics like Father Ralph A. DiOrio of Worcester, Massachusetts, Father Edward McDonough of Boston, and Father Matthew Swizdor of Syracuse, New York, were well established and are now becoming widely accepted even among Catholics who do not consider themselves charismatics.

The renewal of the healing ministry in the Catholic Church, however, is more than a popular movement begun by the charismatics. On the doctrinal level, the Second Vatican Council recommended that the rite of anointing of the sick be restored as a sacrament of healing.

This rite, which had flourished as a sacrament of healing throughout the Church's first eight hundred

149

years, had been gradually transformed during the Middle Ages until it had become a rite of preparation for death. The change reflected a theology which emphasized the importance of soul over the health of the body. Although the Church never denied the healing effect of the sacrament, by the twelfth century the rite was being used almost exclusively as a sacrament for the dying. Those who were anointed weren't expected to be cured; rather, it was intended that the rite would heal their souls of the effects of sin. For this reason, the rite came to be commonly known as "extreme unction" or "the last rites."

In 1551, the Council of Trent affirmed the practice of using the sacrament primarily for the benefit of persons who were dying. It was not until the early 1960s that the Second Vatican Council in its "Constitution on the Sacred Liturgy" decreed that "extreme unction" more fittingly should be called "anointing of the sick" and prescribed it for anyone seriously ill. The fruit of the council's decrees was the restored *Rite of Anointing and Pastoral Care of the Sick* issued by Pope Paul VI in 1972.

The new rite, used with prayers for healing, was issued at a time when the charismatic renewal was growing rapidly in many parts of the world. Catholics therefore were hearing what seemed to be a new message coming both from the charismatic renewal and from the teaching authority of the Church: God heals through prayer. Actually, the message is as old as the Church itself.

The Catholic Church believes as strongly as other

Christian churches do in praying for healing. It also teaches that not only the prayers of the living but also the prayers of saints in heaven are heard and answered by God. For example, Brother André, as we have seen, frequently insisted that it was not his prayers but those of Saint Joseph that made people well.

Miraculous cures have long been viewed by the Church as signs of the sanctity of the departed heroes to whom they were attributed. Part of the official process of beatification and canonization of saints includes the examination of evidence that such cures have occurred. The Church, in fact, has recorded and documented many more healings of that kind than healings attributed to the prayers of living Christians.

Because of space limitations, this book has focused only on Catholics who exercised healing gifts during their lives on earth, and, it must be added, the list of healers mentioned in the book is far from complete. Additional chapters could have been devoted to a number of other individuals, some of them well known and some obscure. Some deserve mention here.

Father Johann Josef Gassner, an Austrian priest of the eighteenth century, is obscure now; but in his own time he attracted a great deal of attention because of his apparent ability to cure the sick. His cures were limited to diseases which he discerned to be of demonic origin, and he cured them by laying hands on the sick and commanding the demons to depart.

Father Gassner's integrity and faith were apparently never seriously questioned, but — like Padre Pio and others — he became embroiled in controversy.

Thousands sought his help, and a circuslike atmosphere grew up around him. Persons unconnected with his ministry began selling oils, powders, and teas which they claimed had been blessed by Father Gassner. Several bishops forbade the healer to "practice" in their dioceses, and finally he was forced to abandon his healing practices and to return to duties as a parish priest.

Saint Jean Baptiste Marie Vianney, also known as the Curé of Ars, was perhaps the best-known Catholic healer of the early nineteenth century. Born in France in 1786, he is better known as a confessor than as a healer. Nevertheless, his reputation as a confessor was built not only on his ability to listen compassionately to sinners but also on the conversions and healings experienced by the penitents whose confessions he heard.

Like Brother André, he was poorly educated, and while he was preparing for the priesthood he did poorly in his studies — especially Latin. His studies were interrupted when he was drafted into Napoleon's army in 1809. He deserted and hid in a mountain village until the following year when a declaration of amnesty was announced. Ordained in 1815 and assigned in 1818 to the village of Ars, he devoted his life to intense prayer and long hours in the confessional. He regularly heard confessions from shortly after midnight until early evening. By 1855, twenty thousand pilgrims a year were journeying to Ars to speak to him.

The humble Curé of Ars sometimes seemed to exhibit a supernatural knowledge both of the past and of the future. He manifested a gift, also shared by Saint Catherine and Padre Pio, of "reading hearts." It was by this gift that he was able to know and understand sins that penitents had committed but had not confessed. And sometimes, like Padre Pio and Father Solanus, he accurately predicted future events. Thousands of healings have been attributed to him, both before and after his death in 1859.

Among other Catholic healers, two English bishops named Saint Cuthbert and John of Beverly were well-known in the seventh century for their healing powers. Saint Vincent de Paul was a Catholic healer of the sixteenth century who, like Catherine of Siena, healed the sick through prayer while caring for them in practical, natural ways as well. Saint Francis Xavier put his extensive knowledge of medicine to good use as a missionary in the Far East, but many of his letters also give details of miraculous cures. The healings of Saint Philip Neri, Saint Francis de Sales, and others are well known.

In examining the lives of Catholic saints who have exercised healing gifts, certain traits appear over and over again. Typically, these healers do not believe that they possess any power to heal. When they are credited with having healed someone, they regularly deny the claim and attribute the cure to God's mercy, to the intercession of the saints, or to the power of Christ in the sacrifice of the Mass.

What they *do* possess is strong faith in *God's* power to heal. Their faith is so strong that it becomes contagious. Peter tells a cripple to stand and walk. The cripple, instead of jeering, is somehow inspired by Peter's faith and makes his own act of faith. He struggles to his feet. By the grace of God, he walks.

If there is a difference between the Catholic healers of the past and the healers of the modern charismatic and Pentecostal movements, it is this: the great healers in the Catholic tradition have recognized that both healing and suffering are part of God's plan; that sometimes, in his own mysterious way, God chooses to work through our acceptance of illness rather than through its healing.

For a Catholic, the suffering of the cross and the joy of the resurrection are complementary parts of our life in Christ. Christ suffered; so if one chooses to follow Christ as fully as possible, one should heed Christ's words, "Whoever wishes to be my follower must deny his very self, take up his cross each day, and follow in my steps" (Luke 9:23).

Repeatedly, the great Catholic healers have, like Christ, gladly embraced suffering in their own lives while praying to remove it from the lives of others. They tend to speak almost lovingly of their suffering as a means of drawing closer to Jesus.

When Father Solanus was dying, a visitor remarked, "You must be hurting quite a bit." The dying priest replied, "Would to God it were ten thousand times worse."

Padre Pio once confided to his confessor that although he wanted God to remove from his hands the visible marks that had appeared there, he had no desire to be free of the pain that came with them. "I will raise my voice," Padre Pio prayed, "and will not cease to implore Him until, in His mercy, He removes, not the wounds or the pain (this is impossible inasmuch as I want to be

154

inebriated with pain), but these visible signs that are an embarrassment and an indescribable humiliation."

To twentieth-century Americans, such attitudes toward pain may seem masochistic and neurotic; but in the lives of the saints, suffering is not an end in itself but a means of redemption closely related to Christ's own suffering on the cross.

"My whole body hurts. Thanks be to God," Father Solanus told his superior the day before he died. "I am offering my sufferings that all might be one. Oh, if I could only live to see the conversion of the whole world."

Among all the great Catholic healers whose stories have been told in this book, there are none who made healing the center of their lives. Rather, they made Christ the center of their lives. They devoted themselves to the Lord. They imitated him. They sought to share his life as fully as they could. In doing so, they grew in their capacity to think as Jesus did, to feel as he did, and to act as he did. They became men and women whose compassion for the poor, the sick, and the needy was the compassion of Jesus Christ.

When they encountered people who were ill and suffering, they grieved for them, just as Jesus did. Tenderly, they stretched out their hands to those people and, like Jesus, prayed lovingly to the Father, asking him to show mercy.

In doing so, they fulfilled Christ's teaching: "I solemnly assure you, the man who has faith in me will do the works I do and greater far than these" (John 14:12).

Catholic healers have been doing the works of

155

Christ for nearly two thousand years. By God's grace our own generation and generations to come will produce new Catholic healers who will continue that tradition until Christ returns.

Bibliography

Angelini, Antonio. "Fr. Solanus Casey, the Man with Unshaken Faith," in *L'Osservatore Romano*, November 24, 1982. Vatican City: L'Osservatore Romano.

Athanasius, Saint. "Life of St. Anthony," in *The Fathers of the Church*. Washington, D.C.: Catholic University of America Press, 1948.

Augustine, Saint. "The City of God," in *The Fathers of the Church*. Washington D.C.: Catholic University of America Press, 1954.

Baldwin, Robert F. *The End of the World: A Catholic View*. Huntington, Ind.: Our Sunday Visitor, 1984.

Barrosse, Thomas, C.S.C. "A Moment of Grace," in *Circular Letter of the Superior General, No. 17*, November 30, 1981. Rome: Congregation of the Holy Cross.

Bornkamm, Gunther. *Paul*, tr. D.M.G. Stalker. New York: Harper and Row Publishers, Inc., 1971.

Brown, Raphael. *The Little Flowers of St. Francis*. Garden City, N.Y.: Image Books, Doubleday and Co., Inc., 1958.

Chadwick, Owen. *Western Asceticism*, Vol. XII. Philadelphia: Westminster Press, 1958.

Champlin, Joseph. *Healing in the Catholic Church: Mending Wounded Hearts and Bodies*. Huntington, Ind.: Our Sunday Visitor, 1985.

Collard, Edgar Andrew. "Brother André and St. Joseph's Shrine," in *L'Oratoire*. Montreal, Que.: St. Joseph's Oratory of Mt. Royal.

Crosby, Michael H., O.F.M. Cap. *Thank God Ahead of Time: The Life and Spirituality of Solanus Casey*. Chicago: Franciscan Herald Press, 1985.

Eban, Abba. *Heritage: Civilization and the Jews*. New York: Summit Books, Simon and Schuster, 1984.

Fullop-Miller, René. *The Saints That Moved the World*. New York: Thomas Y. Crowell Co., 1945.

Gregory the Great, Saint. "Dialogues," in *The Fathers of the Church*. Washington, D.C.: Catholic University of America Press, 1954.

Guimond, John, O.F.M. Cap. *Thanks Be to God: The Spirit and Life of Father Solanus Casey*. Detroit: The Father Solanus Guild, 1978.

Habig, Marion A. *Saint Francis of Assisi: Early Writings and Biographies*. Chicago: Franciscan Herald Press, 1973.

Holmes, J.D. and Bickers, B.W. *A Short History of the Catholic Church*. Ramsey, N.J.: Paulist Press, 1984.

Hughes, Philip. *A Popular History of the Catholic Church*. Garden City, N.Y.: Image Books, Doubleday and Co., Inc., 1954.

Joel, Kenny. "Fr. Capuchin," in *Friar Magazine*, January 1976. Butler, N.J.: Order of Friars Minor.

Jorgensen, Johannes. *Saint Catherine of Siena*, tr. Ingeborg Lund. New York: Longmans, Green and Co., 1938.

Justin Martyr. "Second Apology to the Roman Senate," tr. Thomas B. Falls, in *The Fathers of the Church*. Washington, D.C.: Catholic University of America Press, 1948.

Kelsey, Morton T. *Healing and Christianity*. New York: Harper and Row Publishers, Inc., 1976.

Major, Ralph H. *Faiths That Healed*. New York: D. Appleton-Century Co., 1940.

McKenzie, John L. *Dictionary of the Bible*. New York: Macmillan Publishing Co., Inc., 1965.

Muggeridge, Malcolm and Vidler, Alec. *Paul, Envoy Extraordinary*. New York: Harper and Row Publishers, Inc., 1972.

Nicene and Post-Nicene Fathers, 2nd series. New York: The Christian Literature Co., 1895.

Odell, Catherine. "The Monastery Porter Who May Be America's 20th-Century Saint," in *Our Sunday Visitor*, January 23, 1983. Huntington, Ind.: Our Sunday Visitor.

Roberts, Margaret. *Saint Catherine of Siena and Her Times*. London: Methuen and Co., 1906.

Ruffin, C. Bernard. *Padre Pio: The True Story*. Huntington, Ind.: Our Sunday Visitor, 1982.

Ryley, M. Beresford. *Queens of the Renaissance*. Boston: Small, Maynard and Co., 1907.

Sabatier, P. *Life of St. Francis of Assisi*. New York: L.S. Houghton, 1917.

Sulpicius Severus. "Life of St. Martin," tr. Bernard M.

Peebles, in *The Fathers of the Church*. Washington, D.C.: Catholic University of America Press, 1948.

Tertullian. "To Scapula," tr. Rudolph Arbesmann, in *The Fathers of the Church*. Washington, D.C.: Catholic University of America Press, 1948.